A Note From Rick Renner

I am on a personal quest to see a "revival of the Bible" so people can establish their lives on a firm foundation that will stand strong and endure the test as end-time storm winds begin to intensify.

In order to experience a revival of the Bible in your personal life, it is important to take time each day to read, receive, and apply its truths to your life. James tells us that if we will continue in the perfect law of liberty — refusing to be forgetful hearers, but determined to be doers — we will be blessed in our ways. As you watch or listen to the programs in this series and work through this corresponding study guide, I trust you will search the Scriptures and allow the Holy Spirit to help you hear something new from God's Word that applies specifically to your life. I encourage you to be a doer of the Word He reveals to you. Whatever the cost, I assure you — it will be worth it.

> Thy words were found, and I did eat them;
> and thy word was unto me the joy and rejoicing of mine heart:
> for I am called by thy name, O Lord God of hosts.
> — Jeremiah 15:16

Your brother and friend in Jesus Christ,

Rick Renner

Unless otherwise indicated, all scripture quotations are taken from the *King James Version* of the Bible.

Scripture quotations marked (*AMPC*) are taken from the *Amplified® Bible, Classic Edition*. Copyright © 1954, 1958, 1962, 1964, 1965, 1987 by The Lockman Foundation. Used by permission. www.Lockman.org.

All Scripture marked with the designation (*GW*) is taken from GOD'S WORD®. © 1995, 2003, 2013, 2014, 2019, 2020 by God's Word to the Nations Mission Society. Used by permission.

Scripture quotations marked (*MSG*) are taken from *The Message*, copyright © 1993, 2002, 2018 by Eugene H. Peterson. Used by permission of NavPress. All rights reserved. Represented by Tyndale House Publishers, Inc.

Scripture quotations marked (*NIV*) are taken from the *Holy Bible, New International Version®*, *NIV®* Copyright ©1973, 1978, 1984, 2011 by Biblica, Inc.® Used by permission. All rights reserved worldwide.

Scripture quotations marked (*NKJV*) are taken from the *New King James Version®*. Copyright © 1982 by Thomas Nelson. Used by permission. All rights reserved.

Scripture quotations marked (*NLT*) are taken from the Holy Bible, *New Living Translation*, copyright © 1996, 2004, 2015 by Tyndale House Foundation. Used by permission of Tyndale House Publishers, Inc., Carol Stream, Illinois 60188. All rights reserved.

Scripture quotations marked (*RIV*) are taken from *Renner Interpretive Version*. Copyright © 2021 by Rick Renner.

Scripture quotations marked (*TLB*) are taken from *The Living Bible* copyright © 1971. Used by permission of Tyndale House Publishers, Inc., Carol Stream, Illinois 60188. All rights reserved.

The Protective Promises of Psalm 91
Laying Claim to Every Promise in the Ninety-First Psalm

Copyright © 2023 by Rick Renner
1814 W. Tacoma St.
Broken Arrow, OK 74012-1406

Published by Rick Renner Ministries
www.renner.org

ISBN 13: 978-1-6675-0596-1

eBook ISBN 13: 978-1-6675-0597-8

Printed in the United States of America. All rights reserved. No portion of this book may be reproduced or transmitted in any form or by any means — electronic, mechanical, photocopy, recording, scanning, or other — except for brief quotations in critical reviews or articles, without the prior written permission of the Publisher.

How To Use This Study Guide

This 10-lesson study guide corresponds to *"The Protective Promises of Psalm 91" With Rick Renner* (**Renner TV**). Each lesson in this study guide covers a topic that is addressed during the program series, with questions and references supplied to draw you deeper into your own private study of the Scriptures on this subject.

To derive the most benefit from this study guide, consider the following:

First, watch or listen to the program prior to working through the corresponding lesson in this guide. (Programs can also be viewed at **renner.org** by clicking on the Media/Archives links or on our Renner Ministries YouTube channel.)

Second, take the time to look up the scriptures included in each lesson. Prayerfully consider their application to your own life.

Third, use a journal or notebook to make note of your answers to each lesson's Study Questions and Practical Application challenges.

Fourth, invest specific time in prayer and in the Word of God to consult with the Holy Spirit. Write down the scriptures or insights He reveals to you.

Finally, take action! Whatever the Lord tells you to do according to His Word, do it.

For added insights on this subject, it is recommended that you obtain Vikki Burke's book *Help! It's Dangerous Out Here: How To Walk in Supernatural Protection.* You may also select from Rick's other available resources by placing your order at **renner.org** or by calling 1-800-742-5593.

LESSON 1

TOPIC
Dwelling in the Shadow of the Almighty

SCRIPTURES
1. **Psalm 91:1** — He that dwelleth in the secret place of the most High shall abide under the shadow of the Almighty.
2. **Psalm 32:7** — Thou art my hiding place; thou shalt preserve me from trouble; thou shalt compass me about with songs of deliverance. Selah.
3. **Psalm 27:5** — For in the time of trouble he shall hide me in his pavilion: in the secret of his tabernacle shall he hide me; he shall set me up upon a rock.
4. **Psalm 31:20** — Thou shalt hide them in the secret of thy presence from the pride of man: thou shalt keep them secretly in a pavilion from the strife of tongues.
5. **1 Corinthians 1:30** (*NKJV*) — But… you are in Christ Jesus….
6. **2 Corinthians 5:17** (*NKJV*) — Therefore, if anyone is in Christ, he is a new creation….
7. **Ephesians 1:1** — …To the faithful in Christ Jesus.
8. **Ephesians 1:3** — Blessed be the God and Father of our Lord Jesus Christ, who hath blessed us with all spiritual blessings in heavenly places in Christ.
9. **Ephesians 1:4** (*NKJV*) — Just as He chose us in Him before the foundation of the world….
10. **Ephesians 1:6** — …He hath made us accepted in the beloved.
11. **Ephesians 1:11** — In whom also we have obtained an inheritance….
12. **Ephesians 2:22** — In whom ye also are builded together for an habitation of God through the Spirit.
13. **Colossians 2:10** — And ye are complete in him, which is the head of all principality and power.
14. **1 John 4:15** — Whosoever shall confess that Jesus is the Son of God, God dwelleth in him, and he in God.

15. **Colossians 3:3** — For ye are dead, and your life is hid with Christ in God.
16. **Psalm 17:8** — Keep me as the apple of the eye, hide me under the shadow of thy wings.

GREEK WORDS

No Greek words were shown on the TV program.

SYNOPSIS

The ten lessons in this study, *The Protective Promises of Psalm 91*, will focus on the following topics:

- Dwelling in the Shadow of the Almighty
- What Are You Saying?
- 'You Are My Refuge and Fortress'
- Delivered From the Snare of the Fowler and the Noisome Pestilence
- Covered With God's Feathers and Safe Under His Wings
- His Truth, Your Shield and Buckler — No Fear of the Terror by Night or the Arrow That Flieth by Day
- I Will Not Fear the Pestilence That Walks in Darkness or the Destruction That Wastes at Noonday
- No Evil Shall Befall Thee, Neither Shall Any Plague Come Nigh Thy Dwelling
- He Shall Give His Angels Charge Over Thee To Keep Thee and Bear Thee Up in Their Hands
- God Says: I'll Give You Victory Over All the Works of the Enemy, Satisfy You With Long Life, and Show You My Salvation!

The Ninety-First Psalm is powerful, and it plays a vital part in our lives as believers — especially in these last days. According to historical sources, we understand that Psalms 90 and 91 were written by Moses when the children of Israel were wandering through the wilderness for 40 years after God had delivered them from Egyptian bondage.

Remember, the Israelites had been enslaved in Egypt for 400 years. Through many supernatural signs and wonders, the One True God defeated the gods of Egypt and set His people free to worship and serve

Him. When Moses wrote Psalm 91, the children of Israel were facing all kinds of opposition that they had never experienced before.

When they entered the wilderness, their walk of faith began. For the first time, they were confronting things like wild animals, ferocious beasts, snakes, and scorpions — along with having to trust God for daily provisions of water and food. That's when Moses wrote this psalm, which begins by saying "He that dwelleth in the secret place of the most High shall abide under the shadow of the Almighty" (Psalm 91:1).

What is "the secret place of the Most High," and how do we "abide under the shadow of the Almighty?" In this lesson, we'll answer these and other vital questions concerning Psalm 91:1.

The emphasis of this lesson:

To activate and take hold of God's protective promises in Psalm 91, we must be people who permanently dwell with Him in the "secret place." This is a place of safety and concealment where we are hidden deep inside Christ Jesus — and there is no safer place on the planet.

What Does It Mean To 'Dwell in the Secret Place'?

Psalm 91:1 says, "He that dwelleth in the secret place of the most High shall abide under the shadow of the Almighty." The word "dwelleth" in the original Hebrew here means *to dwell; to lodge; to take up residency;* or *to move into a place and stay there permanently.*

This word "dwelleth" doesn't describe a visitor who comes and goes. Instead, it depicts a person who has taken up permanent residency in one place. He's dwelling, lodging, and taking up permanent residency in the secret place of the Most High.

It's in this first verse that we see the foundational condition for activating and taking hold of God's promises in Psalm 91: we must be people who permanently dwell and live with Him in the "secret place." In Hebrew, the words "secret place" describe *an inner chamber, a place of concealment, a hiding place,* or *a place of secrecy.* It denotes *the most secret compartment.*

This lets us know that there is a secret place in the Lord, and it is a place where we are concealed and hidden in His presence. This place of divine secrecy is available to those who permanently dwell with God. He is a habitation for those who fear Him and walk with Him. As believers, we are hidden deep inside Christ who is in God, which we will learn more about as we go further.

The 'Secret Place' Is Described Throughout the Psalms

The best commentary on the Bible *is* the Bible, and when it comes to understanding the secret place, there are many references throughout Scripture that talk about this fortified place of safety — especially in the book of Psalms. Consider what David wrote in these passages:

In **Psalm 32:7**, he said, "Thou art my hiding place; thou shalt preserve me from trouble; thou shalt compass me about with songs of deliverance. Selah." Here, God is depicted as our *hiding place*, which is one of the definitions of the *secret place*.

In **Psalm 27:5**, David declared, "For in the time of trouble he shall hide me in his pavilion: in the secret of his tabernacle shall he hide me; he shall set me up upon a rock." God's pavilion is the secret place of His tabernacle — the place He invites us to live with Him.

In **Psalm 31:20**, David said, "Thou shalt hide them in the secret of thy presence from the pride of man: thou shalt keep them secretly in a pavilion from the strife of tongues." Here again, we see that the secret place is where we are hidden, concealed, and protected in divine secrecy. This verse says that we are specifically protected from the pride of man. Those who operate in arrogance have little to no fear of God and feel they can get away with anything they want. God keeps us from this.

As a Christian, Your Secret Place Is 'in Christ'

As believers in Jesus, the Bible states that our secret place is *in Christ*. The original Greek text literally says we are "locked up in the Person of Jesus." We can't get tucked away in God any deeper than being *in Christ*. Again and again, the New Testament says we are "in Christ" or "in Him." Take these verses, for example:

- **First Corinthians 1:30** (*NKJV*) says, "But… you are *in Christ Jesus*.…"

- **Second Corinthians 5:17** (*NKJV*) declares, "Therefore, if anyone is *in Christ*, he is a new creation; old things have passed away; behold, all things have become new."
- **Ephesians 1:1** is addressed to, "...The faithful *in Christ Jesus*."
- **Ephesians 1:3** states, "Blessed be the God and Father of our Lord Jesus Christ, who hath blessed us with all spiritual blessings in heavenly places *in Christ*."
- **Ephesians 1:4** (*NKJV*) reveals that "...He [God] chose us *in Him* before the foundation of the world...."
- **Ephesians 1:6** adds that "...He [God] hath made us accepted *in the beloved*." The "beloved" is Jesus. Thus, we are accepted in Christ, the *beloved* of God.
- **Ephesians 1:11** continues the explanation of what is ours in Christ, telling us, "*In whom* also we have obtained an inheritance...." Because we are in Christ, all God's promises are activated in our lives.
- **Ephesians 2:22** states that we are all collectively in Jesus — "*In whom* ye also are builded together for an habitation of God through the Spirit."
- **Colossians 2:10** powerfully declares, "And ye are complete *in him* [Christ] which is the head of all principality and power."
- And in **First John 4:15**, we are told, "Whosoever shall confess that Jesus is the Son of God, God dwelleth in him, and he *in God*." Wow! What a promise! Anyone who confesses that Jesus is the Son of God opens the door of their life for the fullness of God's Spirit to enter and live! God lives in us, and we live in God.

Lastly, we read **Colossians 3:3**, which says, "For ye are dead, and your life is hid *with Christ in God*." Before you were saved, you were spiritually dead in your sins. But the moment you confessed that Jesus is God's Son and believed He died to pay the price for your sin, you were born again, and your new life is hidden in Christ. You can't get any deeper in God than that!

Friend, God wants you to permanently dwell in Christ, which is *in Him*. That is what it means to dwell in the secret place of the Most High.

Stop *Wrestling* and Begin *Resting* in Christ

On the program, Rick candidly shared how when he first came to Christ in his youth, he struggled with his salvation. For quite some time he vacillated, wondering whether or not he was truly saved. He kept trying to get into Christ, not realizing he was already safely tucked away in Him.

It just seems too easy to believe that I've been placed into the Person of Christ, he thought. *Certainly, I'm not saved. It just can't be that simple.* Plagued with the fear that his confession wasn't enough, he would pray a prayer for salvation again and again, saying, "Lord, just in case I didn't really mean it the last time, I'm going to ask You again to forgive me of all my sins and come live inside of me. In Jesus' name."

Finally, a day came when Rick said to the Lord, "I've had enough of this. If I've prayed for You to save me once, I've prayed for You to save me 10,000 times. I don't know how to ask any better or more sincerely; I don't know how to declare You to be the Lord of my life more effectively than I already have. So, Jesus, this is it; I'm not asking anymore. Either I'm saved or I'm not."

In that moment, something wonderful happened. Rick quit wrestling and began to rest in his salvation. From that time on, he never again doubted that he is saved. He began to trust God and believe by faith that he had been placed into the Person of Jesus Christ.

If you've been struggling to believe you are truly saved, God wants that struggle to end today. If you have called on the name of the Lord — confessing with your mouth and believing in your heart that Jesus IS the Son of God who died to pay for your sins and break sin's power over your life, you are saved — period. It's a done deal!

The moment you call Jesus the Lord of your life, the Bible says the Holy Spirit baptizes you — or places you into — the Person of Christ. He is your secret place, and there is no greater hiding place or place of concealment in this life than to be in Him. Indeed, the devil cannot touch you when you're placed in Christ. So breathe easy and rest in Him.

Abide in God's Shadow and He'll Be Your Supreme Protector

Looking once more at Psalm 91:1, it says, "He that dwelleth in the secret place of the most High shall abide under the shadow of the Almighty." It's important to note that the Hebrew word for "Most High" is *Elyon*, which means *The One Who Is Supreme*. It echoes what Paul wrote about Jesus in Colossians 2:10 where he said that Christ is "the head of all principality and power."

If you're saved and "in Christ," you are complete in Him, *The One Who Is Supreme* above all. That means you're complete in Him who has authority over every foul force and every vicious, invisible power in Heaven and earth. Jesus is the Head of all of it!

When you choose to take up permanent residency in the Most High, Scripture says, "…[You] shall abide under the shadow of the Almighty" (Psalm 91:1). The phrase "shall abide" in Hebrew means *to abide, dwell, lodge,* or *reside*. This is what you are called to do — *abide* at the Lord's side. When you're abiding, you are relaxed and enjoying your place in Christ Jesus.

The fact that the Bible says we abide in the *shadow* of the Almighty is significant. That word "shadow" describes *a shelter* or *a hiding place* and denotes *one who stays in step with the Lord*. Think about it: In order to walk in someone's shadow, you have to be very close to him. If he moves, you have to move with him, and you must move in the same direction at the same pace. Otherwise, you will soon be out of his shadow.

Take your time and really absorb what this means because it is the foundation to receiving the divine promises of Psalm 91. Not everyone can lay claim to these verses. Only those who permanently dwell in the secret place and abide close to the Lord — in His shadow — are eligible to inherit these promises.

This brings us to the word "Almighty"— the Hebrew word *Shaddai*, which means *Great Provider* and *One Who Overpowers* everything and everyone else. When you're walking in the shadow of the Lord, you're abiding in the One who has the ability to overcome any evil entity or force that would ever try to assault your life.

Psalm 17:8 says, "Keep me as the apple of the eye, hide me under the shadow of thy wings." Like Psalm 91:1, this verse refers to the divine protection that God provides for those who walk closely with Him. Therefore, if you walk close to the Lord, He will be a refuge and a hiding place to you. In Him, you shall abide under the defense and protection of the Almighty.

STUDY QUESTIONS

> Study to shew thyself approved unto God, a workman that needeth not to be ashamed, rightly dividing the word of truth.
> — 2 Timothy 2:15

1. What new understanding have you gained regarding the background or history of Psalm 91? How about the meaning of the *secret place*?
2. As believers in Jesus, the Bible states that our secret place is *in Christ*. The New Testament is filled with verses confirming this truth. Carefully read these passages, and in your own words, describe the *blessings* you are given as you dwell in relationship with Jesus.
   - 2 Corinthians 5:17
   - 2 Corinthians 5:21
   - Romans 8:1,2
   - Ephesians 1:3-6
   - Ephesians 1:11-14
   - Colossians 2:9,10 and John 1:16

PRACTICAL APPLICATION

> But be ye doers of the word, and not hearers only, deceiving your own selves.
> — James 1:22

1. Rick candidly shared how when he first came to Christ, he struggled to believe that He was truly saved. How about you? Are you vacillating in your faith, wondering whether you are saved and *in Christ*? How is this teaching dispelling fear and helping you know without question that you are saved and securely placed in Jesus? (Also consider Ephesians 2:1-10.)

2. Did you know that Jesus is the HEAD over all power and authority? That is what the name "Most High" (*Elyon*) means, and it is closely connected with the name "Almighty" (*Shaddai*), which means *Great Provider* and *One Who Overpowers* everything and everyone else. How does knowing you are in Christ — the Supreme One over everything — encourage your faith and give you hope? (As you answer, take time to reflect on Ephesians 1:19-23; 4:15; Colossians 1:15-24; First Peter 3:22.)

LESSON 2

TOPIC

What Are You Saying?

SCRIPTURES

1. **Psalm 91:1-16** — He that dwelleth in the secret place of the most High shall abide under the shadow of the Almighty. I will say of the Lord, He is my refuge and my fortress: my God; in him will I trust. Surely he shall deliver thee from the snare of the fowler, and from the noisome pestilence. He shall cover thee with his feathers, and under his wings shalt thou trust: his truth shall be thy shield and buckler. Thou shalt not be afraid for the terror by night; nor for the arrow that flieth by day; nor for the pestilence that walketh in darkness; nor for the destruction that wasteth at noonday. A thousand shall fall at thy side, and ten thousand at thy right hand; but it shall not come nigh thee. Only with thine eyes shalt thou behold and see the reward of the wicked. Because thou hast made the Lord, which is my refuge, even the most High, thy habitation; there shall no evil befall thee, neither shall any plague come nigh thy dwelling. For he shall give his angels charge over thee, to keep thee in all thy ways. They shall bear thee up in their hands, lest thou dash thy foot against a stone. Thou shalt tread upon the lion and adder: the young lion and the dragon shalt thou trample under feet. Because he hath set his love upon me, therefore will I deliver him: I will set him on high, because he hath known my name. He shall call upon me, and I will answer him: I will be with him in trouble; I will deliver him, and honour him. With long life will I satisfy him, and shew him my salvation.

GREEK WORDS
No Greek words were shown on the TV program.

SYNOPSIS
If you've read Psalm 91, you know the promises it contains are wonderful. What you may not know is that they are not automatically activated in your life just because you are a Christian. They are activated when we dwell in the secret place, which is our position in Christ. As we abide in His shadow — staying as close to Him as we can in a loving relationship — we can lay claim to every promise in Psalm 91.

The emphasis of this lesson:

A major key to experiencing the divine protection of Psalm 91 is to personalize and proclaim each verse out loud to the Lord and speak them over ourselves and our loved ones.

A Review of Lesson 1

Moses Wrote Psalm 91. In our first lesson, we learned that Psalms 90 and 91 were written by Moses as he was leading the children of Israel through the wilderness of Sinai. For 400 years prior to that time, the Israelites had been slaves in Egypt, so the territory through which they were walking was totally new. They had left what was familiar, predictable, and in some ways comfortable and were now confronting things they had never experienced — like brute beasts, wild animals, snakes, and scorpions. In the midst of many trying and even terrifying situations, Moses wrote the protective promises of Psalm 91, which begins by saying, "He that dwelleth in the secret place of the most High shall abide under the shadow of the Almighty" (v. 1).

The Word "Dwelleth." In Hebrew, this word means *to dwell, to lodge*, or *to take up residency*. It depicts one who moves into a place and stays there permanently. For us who are believers, this is a picture of taking up permanent residency in Jesus the moment we got saved. First Corinthians 12:13 says, "For by one Spirit are we all baptized into one body, whether we be Jews or Gentiles...." The "one body" mentioned here is *the Body of Christ*, and He is our secret place where we are called to permanently live.

Friend, if you're saved, you're in Christ, and you can relax because you are deeply tucked away in the secret place of the Person of Jesus. He is your hiding place and your place of concealment, and in Him, there is great protection.

A Tragic Dilemma. There are many Christians who begin in Christ, but as time passes and challenges arise, they wander away from the Lord. Because they are no longer dwelling in close fellowship with Him, they can no longer claim the promises of Psalm 91. Those promises are only available to those "…that dwelleth in the secret place of the most High…" (Psalm 91:1).

The verse goes on to say that those who remain in close relationship with the Lord "…shall abide under the shadow of the Almighty" (v. 1). The phrase "shall abide" in Hebrew means to *abide, dwell, lodge,* or *reside*. These promises belong to anyone who abides under the *shadow* of the Almighty. Moreover, we saw that the word "shadow" describes *a shelter* or *a hiding place* and denotes *one who stays in step with the Lord*.

Stay in God's Shadow. If you're going to walk in someone's shadow, you're going to have to stay very close and in step with that person because his or her shadow only extends so far. If you don't walk right alongside that person — going in the same direction at the same pace — eventually, you will move out of his or her shadow. The same is true of your walk with God. To stay in His shadow, you must stay close and in step with Him. Only in this position of intimacy can you claim and experience the promises of Psalm 91.

The Lord Is the "Almighty." In Psalm 91:1, the word "Almighty" is the Hebrew word *Shaddai*, and it means *Great Provider* and *One Who Overpowers*. When you're abiding in the shadow of the Almighty — staying in step with Him and moving in the same direction He is moving — you are abiding and residing in the shelter of the Great Provider and the One Who Overpowers everything and everyone else!

Speaking God's Promises Is Essential To Experiencing Them

When we come to Psalm 91:2, it says, "I will say of the Lord, He is my refuge and my fortress: my God; in him will I trust." Like verse 1, understanding this second verse is key to experiencing all the promises that follow. What is very interesting about this passage is that in the original Hebrew, the opening phrase is not "I will say of the Lord." It is "I will say *TO* the Lord." This tells us clearly:

Psalm 91 is a *confession* — or *declaration* — of faith.

To claim and experience these promises of God, we have to put them in our mouth and speak them out loud to the Lord. It is not enough just to think about them or believe them; we must vocally declare these promises to God and speak them over our life in order to activate them. This demonstrates the inseparable connection between faith and speaking.

Faith always speaks — it never just thinks.

This principle is made clear in Second Corinthians 4:13, which says, "We having the same spirit of faith, according as it is written, I believed, and therefore have I spoken; we also believe, and therefore speak." Notice that the verse doesn't say, "I believed, and therefore I *think*." Instead, it says, "I believed, and therefore have I *spoken*." This tells us that when we truly believe something, we need to be speaking it with our mouth. The real power of faith is not released until words of faith are released from our mouth.

Jesus said, "For verily I say unto you, That whosoever shall *say* unto this mountain, Be thou removed, and be thou cast into the sea; and shall not doubt in his heart, but shall believe that those things which he *saith* shall come to pass; he shall have whatsoever he *saith*" (Mark 11:23). Again, notice that Jesus didn't say, "…Whosoever shall *think* about this mountain." He said, "…Whosoever shall *say* unto this mountain." In fact, the word *say* or *saith* appears in this verse three times!

Mountain-moving power is released through your mouth, not your mind.

Yes, renewing your mind with God's Word is essential, but it is speaking God's Word with your mouth that detonates His dynamic strength. When you believe something and speak it out of your mouth — and don't doubt in your heart — Jesus said it will come to pass.

The word "doubt" is the Greek word *diakrino*, and it depicts *one who is doubtful or one who wavers back and forth*. This is a person who is constantly changing his mind about what he believes, going back and forth and wobbling in his faith. This word "doubt" (*diakrino*) would be better translated *differ*. Hence, we could translate Jesus' words in Mark 11:23, "...Whosoever shall say unto this mountain, Be thou removed, and be thou cast into the sea; and shall not *differ in his heart*, but shall believe that those things which he saith shall come to pass; he shall have whatsoever he saith."

This tells us plainly that our heart and our mouth have to be saying the same thing. If you're saying one thing with your mouth, but you don't believe it in your heart, it's not going to manifest. You have to get your mouth and heart into agreement. That's why you need to be working on your heart all the time.

With regards to Psalm 91, you have to plant each verse in your heart, and once they're in your heart, you have to get them in your mouth. There can be no differing confession between your heart and your mouth. When your heart and mouth line up, then you can declare God's promises and experience all that He has for you. The words of your mouth set the course for your life.

Personalize Psalm 91 and SAY IT to the Lord

To help you grasp the idea of speaking God's promises, let's go through Psalm 91 verse by verse — reading what the scripture says and then making it a personal confession.

Psalm 91:1 says, "He that dwelleth in the secret place of the most High shall abide under the shadow of the Almighty." When we personalize this passage, it says:

> *I dwell in the secret place of the Most High; I abide in the shadow of the Almighty.*

Psalm 91:2 says, "I will say of the Lord, He is my refuge and my fortress: my God; in him will I trust." When we personalize this verse, we have a confession of faith that states:

> *I will say to You, Lord: You are my refuge; You are my fortress; You are my God. I trust in You.*

Psalm 91:3 says, "Surely he shall deliver thee from the snare of the fowler, and from the noisome pestilence." When we personalize this verse, we have a confession of faith that declares:

You will deliver me from the snare of the fowler; You will deliver me from noisome pestilence.

Psalm 91:4 says, "He shall cover thee with his feathers, and under his wings shalt thou trust: his truth shall be thy shield and buckler." When we personalize this verse, we have a confession of faith that states:

You cover me with Your feathers; You put me safely under Your wings. Your truth is my shield and buckler.

Psalm 91:5 says, "Thou shalt not be afraid for the terror by night; nor for the arrow that flieth by day. When we personalize this verse, we have a confession of faith that declares:

I will not be afraid of the terror by night; I will not be afraid of the arrow that flies by day.

Psalm 91:6 says, "Nor for the pestilence that walketh in darkness; nor for the destruction that wasteth at noonday." When we personalize this verse, we have a confession of faith that proclaims:

I will not fear pestilence that walks in darkness; I will not fear destruction that wastes at noonday.

Psalm 91:7 says, "A thousand shall fall at thy side, and ten thousand at thy right hand; but it shall not come nigh thee." When we personalize this verse, we have a confession of faith that states:

A thousand will fall at my side, and ten thousand at my right hand, but it will not come nigh me.

Psalm 91:8 says, "Only with thine eyes shalt thou behold and see the reward of the wicked." When we personalize this verse, we have a confession of faith that declares:

Only with my eyes will I behold the reward of the wicked.

Psalm 91:9 says, "Because thou hast made the Lord, which is my refuge, even the most High, thy habitation." When we personalize this verse, we have a confession of faith that proclaims:

I have made the Lord my refuge; I have made the Most High my habitation.

Psalm 91:10 says, "There shall no evil befall thee, neither shall any plague come nigh thy dwelling." When we personalize this verse, we have a confession of faith that states:

> *No evil will befall me; no plague will come nigh my dwelling.*

Psalm 91:11 says, "For he shall give his angels charge over thee, to keep thee in all thy ways." When we personalize this verse, we have a confession of faith that declares:

> *You give Your angels charge over me to keep me in all my ways.*

Psalm 91:12 says, "They shall bear thee up in their hands, lest thou dash thy foot against a stone." When we personalize this verse, we have a confession of faith that proclaims:

> *Your angels bear me up in their hands, lest I dash my foot against a stone.*

Psalm 91:13 says, "Thou shalt tread upon the lion and adder: the young lion and the dragon shalt thou trample under feet." When we personalize this verse, we have a confession of faith that states:

> *I will tread upon the lion and the adder; I trample the young lion and dragon under my feet.*

In **Psalm 91:14**, God is speaking, and He says, "Because he hath set his love upon me, therefore will I deliver him: I will set him on high, because he hath known my name." When we personalize this passage, we have a confession of faith that declares:

> *I have set my love upon Him; You deliver me, and You set me on High.*

In **Psalm 91:15**, God continues His declaration over you saying, "He shall call upon me, and I will answer him: I will be with him in trouble; I will deliver him, and honour him." When we personalize this verse, we have a confession of faith that proclaims:

> *I call upon You, and You answer me. You are with me in trouble; You deliver me, and You honor me.*

Psalm 91:16 is the final verse of the chapter, in which God says, "With long life will I satisfy him, and shew him my salvation." When we personalize this passage, we have a confession of faith that states:

With long life You satisfy me, and You show me Your salvation.

Friend, if you want these promises of Psalm 91 to be activated in your life, you have to do more than just think about them — you need to believe them in your heart and speak them out of your mouth. In our next lesson, we will learn what is meant when the Bible says that God is "my refuge and my fortress" (*see* Psalm 91:3).

STUDY QUESTIONS

> Study to shew thyself approved unto God, a workman that needeth not to be ashamed, rightly dividing the word of truth.
> — 2 Timothy 2:15

1. Mountain-moving power is released through your *mouth*, not your mind. How powerful are your words? Read what God says in James 3:2-5; Proverbs 18:20 and 21; and Proverbs 13:2 and 3. Also consider what He says about the *mouth of the righteous* in Psalm 37:30 and 31; and Proverbs 10:11,13,20,21,31 and 32.

2. Make no mistake: renewing your mind with God's Word is vital, but it is speaking His Word with your mouth that detonates His dynamic power. Jeremiah 23:28 (*AMPC*) says, "...He who has My word, let him speak My word faithfully...." According to the verses below, what can you expect to happen when you consistently speak God's Word in prayer?
   - Jeremiah 23:28,29
   - Hebrews 4:12
   - James 1:21-25 and Romans 1:16
   - Ezekiel 37:1-14

PRACTICAL APPLICATION

> But be ye doers of the word, and not hearers only, deceiving your own selves.
> — James 1:22

1. To experience the promises of God in Psalm 91, we have to plant them in our heart and speak them with our mouth. Thinking about and meditating on Scripture is good and needed, but to activate God's

Word, we must declare His truth out loud — *to God, over ourselves and loved ones*, and *against the enemy*. Are you actively doing this in your life? If not, what's keeping you from it?

2. Our heart and our mouth have to be saying the same thing. If we're saying one thing with our mouth but don't believe it in our heart, it's not going to manifest. If you want to see your mouth and heart get into agreement, begin to pray: *Lord, please help me to regularly hide Your Word in my heart. Do a work in my life that causes my heart and mouth to come into agreement with Your Word. And help me speak Your Word faithfully. In Jesus' name. Amen!*

LESSON 3

TOPIC

'You Are My Refuge and Fortress'

SCRIPTURES

1. **Psalm 91:1-16** — He that dwelleth in the secret place of the most High shall abide under the shadow of the Almighty. I will say of the Lord, He is my refuge and my fortress: my God; in him will I trust. Surely he shall deliver thee from the snare of the fowler, and from the noisome pestilence. He shall cover thee with his feathers, and under his wings shalt thou trust: his truth shall be thy shield and buckler. Thou shalt not be afraid for the terror by night; nor for the arrow that flieth by day; nor for the pestilence that walketh in darkness; nor for the destruction that wasteth at noonday. A thousand shall fall at thy side, and ten thousand at thy right hand; but it shall not come nigh thee. Only with thine eyes shalt thou behold and see the reward of the wicked. Because thou hast made the Lord, which is my refuge, even the most High, thy habitation; there shall no evil befall thee, neither shall any plague come nigh thy dwelling. For he shall give his angels charge over thee, to keep thee in all thy ways. They shall bear thee up in their hands, lest thou dash thy foot against a stone. Thou shalt tread upon the lion and adder: the young lion and the dragon shalt thou trample under feet. Because he hath set his love upon me, therefore will I deliver him: I will set him on high, because he hath known my name. He shall call upon me, and I will answer him: I will be with

him in trouble; I will deliver him, and honour him. With long life will I satisfy him, and shew him my salvation.
2. **Deuteronomy 33:27** — The eternal God is thy refuge, and underneath are the everlasting arms....
3. **2 Samuel 22:2** — ...The Lord is my rock, and my fortress, and my deliverer.
4. **Psalm 18:2** — The Lord is my rock, and my fortress, and my deliverer; my God, my strength, in whom I will trust; my buckler, and the horn of my salvation, and my high tower.
5. **Psalm 27:5** — For in the time of trouble he shall hide me in his pavilion: in the secret of his tabernacle shall he hide me; he shall set me up upon a rock.
6. **Psalm 31:20** — Thou shalt hide them in the secret of thy presence from the pride of man: thou shalt keep them secretly in a pavilion from the strife of tongues.
7. **Psalm 46:1** — God is our refuge and strength, a very present help in trouble.
8. **Psalm 62:6** — He only is my rock and my salvation: he is my defence; I shall not be moved.
9. **Psalm 71:3** — Be thou my strong habitation, whereunto I may continually resort: thou hast given commandment to save me; for thou art my rock and my fortress.
10. **Psalm 144:2** — My goodness, and my fortress; my high tower, and my deliverer; my shield, and he in whom I trust....
11. **Proverbs 14:26** — In the fear of the Lord is strong confidence: and his children shall have a place of refuge.
12. **Nahum 1:7** — The Lord is good, a strong hold in the day of trouble; and he knoweth them that trust in him.

GREEK WORDS

No Greek words were shown on the TV program.

SYNOPSIS

The world today is a very different place than it was just a few years ago. It seems we are engulfed by unprecedented dangers and troubling situations. Rather than run and hide, God is calling us to rise and shine! We are His

Church — the Blood-bought, Blood-washed, sanctified, and set-apart children of God. As we abide in Christ, who is our *secret place*, God has given us the promise of divine protection, which is detailed in Psalm 91. Instead of just reading or thinking about these verses, we are to declare them out loud to the Lord — *and* over our lives. Indeed, He is our Refuge and our Fortress in these last of the last days!

The emphasis of this lesson:

God has promised to be your Refuge — a shelter from all kinds of dangerous storms and situations. He is also committed to being your Fortress — a stronghold of defense and protection. He wants you to put absolute confidence and trust in Him.

What We Know So Far

Psalms 90 and 91 are understood to have been written by Moses at the time he was leading the children of Israel in the wilderness of Sinai. For more than 400 years prior to that time, the descendants of Israel had been enslaved by the Egyptians and forced to build the cities of the ancient Pharaohs. But through the amazing, demonstrated power of God, Israel was delivered from bondage and free to worship the One True God.

Much to their surprise, their freedom brought with it unexpected problems, like ferocious wild beasts, snakes, scorpions, and numerous enemies. When Israel was faced with many fears, Moses wrote Psalm 91, declaring to his people, "He that dwelleth in the secret place of the most High shall abide under the shadow of the Almighty" (v. 1). Without question, there is no safer place on the planet than living in the shadow of the Almighty!

Understanding Psalm 91:1 is vital to experiencing the promises outlined in the remainder of the chapter. Here again are the meanings of some of the key words in this verse:

"Dwelleth" — In Hebrew, this word means *to dwell, to lodge,* or *to take up residency*. It carries the idea of moving into a place and staying there permanently. Where is it that we are to move and take up permanent residency? God said the *secret place*.

"Secret place" — In Hebrew, this describes *an inner chamber, a place of concealment, a hiding place,* or *a place of secrecy*. It denotes *the most secret compartment*. For believers, this is being *in Christ*, which we examined in

Lesson 1. The moment we were saved, we were placed in Christ, and He became our place of permanent residency.

"Most High" — This is the Hebrew word *Elyon*, which means *The One Who Is Supreme*. That is the God you serve — *The One Who Is Supreme* and able to defeat any foe that comes against you!

"Shall abide" — In Hebrew, this means *to abide, dwell, lodge*, or *reside*. We are called to *abide* or *live* in the "shadow of the Almighty." We are not called to visit God's presence on Sundays, Wednesdays, and on special occasions. We are called to make the Lord our place of permanent residency.

"Shadow" — This word describes *a shelter* or *a hiding place*. Specifically, it denotes *one who stays in step with the Lord*. As we have noted in previous lessons, to abide in someone's shadow requires us to stay very close to him. When he moves, we move. If he stops, we stop. Again, to stay in his shadow is to stay in step with him, which is precisely what God is calling us to do with Him, and it is a requirement for experiencing the protective promises of Psalm 91.

What Does 'Abiding in the Shadow of the Almighty' Look Like?

If you have asked this question, the answer can be summed up in two words: *building relationship*. Abiding in the shadow of the Almighty is all about *building relationship* with Him. This includes the life-giving practice of beginning each day with prayer, reading and studying Scripture, and spending time worshiping God and sitting in His presence. He is thrilled when you give Him your undivided attention — especially before you begin your daily routine and work.

It's during this time you really want to pause and examine your life, asking the Holy Spirit to search your heart and reveal what's going on inside (*see* Psalm 139:23,24). In His love, He will reveal wrong attitudes, hidden sin, offense and unforgiveness, and show you if you have gotten off track and are deviating from your destiny. If you ask Him, He will even show you any changes that He wants you to make to remain in step with Him.

Remember, when you abide in the shadow of the Almighty, you have great protection. The Hebrew word for "Almighty" here is the word *Shaddai*, which means *Great Provider* and *One Who Overpowers*. When you live in the shadow of the Almighty, you're living in the supernatural shelter of the One who will provide everything you need and overpower any enemy that would try to come against you.

The Promises of Psalm 91

In addition to dwelling in the secret place of the Most High and abiding in His shadow, there is something else we need to do in order to activate the promises of Psalm 91, and it is found in verse 2. It says, "I will say of the Lord, He is my refuge and my fortress: my God; in him will I trust." We learned in Lesson 2 that the original Greek text of this verse actually says, "I will say TO the Lord…." This tells us clearly that Psalm 91 is a *confession* — or *declaration* — of faith.

Here again is Psalm 91 in its entirety:

> **He that dwelleth in the secret place of the most High shall abide under the shadow of the Almighty.**
>
> **I will say of the Lord, He is my refuge and my fortress: my God; in him will I trust.**
>
> **Surely he shall deliver thee from the snare of the fowler, and from the noisome pestilence.**
>
> **He shall cover thee with his feathers, and under his wings shalt thou trust: his truth shall be thy shield and buckler.**
>
> **Thou shalt not be afraid for the terror by night; nor for the arrow that flieth by day;**
>
> **Nor for the pestilence that walketh in darkness; nor for the destruction that wasteth at noonday.**
>
> **A thousand shall fall at thy side, and ten thousand at thy right hand; but it shall not come nigh thee.**
>
> **Only with thine eyes shalt thou behold and see the reward of the wicked.**
>
> **Because thou hast made the Lord, which is my refuge, even the most High, thy habitation;**
>
> **There shall no evil befall thee, neither shall any plague come nigh thy dwelling.**

For he shall give his angels charge over thee, to keep thee in all thy ways.

They shall bear thee up in their hands, lest thou dash thy foot against a stone.

Thou shalt tread upon the lion and adder: the young lion and the dragon shalt thou trample under feet.

Because he hath set his love upon me, therefore will I deliver him: I will set him on high, because he hath known my name.

He shall call upon me, and I will answer him: I will be with him in trouble; I will deliver him, and honour him.

With long life will I satisfy him, and shew him my salvation.

To claim and experience these promises of God, we have to believe them in our heart *and* put them in our mouth. It is not enough just to *think* about them — we must also declare aloud to God and speak them over our life in order to activate them. Faith always speaks — it never just thinks. There is an inseparable connection between faith and speaking. With that in mind, here is the personalized version of Psalm 91:

Your Personal Declaration of Psalm 91

I dwell in the secret place of the Most High.
I abide in the shadow of the Almighty.
You are my refuge.
You are my fortress.
You are my God.
I trust in You.
You will deliver me from the snare of the fowler.
You will deliver me from noisome pestilence.
You cover me with Your feathers.
You put me safely under Your wings.
Your truth is my shield and buckler.
I will not be afraid of the terror by night.
I will not be afraid of the arrow that flieth by day.
I will not fear pestilence that walks in darkness.
I will not fear destruction that wastes at noonday.

The Protective Promises of Psalm 91 | 25

A thousand will fall at my side,
and ten thousand at my right hand, but it will not come nigh me.
Only with my eyes will I behold the reward of the wicked.
I have made the Lord my refuge.
I have made the Most High my habitation.
No evil will befall me.
No plague will come nigh my dwelling.
You give Your angels charge over me to keep me in all my ways.
Your angels bear me up in their hands,
lest I dash my foot against a stone.
I will tread upon the lion and the adder.
I trample the young lion and dragon under my feet.
I have set my love upon Him.
You deliver me.
You set me on High.
I call upon You, and You answer me.
You are with me in trouble.
You deliver me.
You honor me.
With long life You satisfy me.
You show me Your salvation.

This is your declaration of faith that you are to make to the Lord. The fact that it is personalized helps you realize this is not just something God is going to do for someone else — it is what He has promised to do for *you*! So along with hiding Psalm 91 in your heart, personalize it and put it in your mouth.

The Lord Is Your 'Refuge' and 'Fortress' in Times of Trouble

Looking once more at Psalm 91:2, it says, "I will say of the Lord, He is my refuge and my fortress: my God; in him will I trust." Notice it says that God is your "refuge." This is a translation of a Hebrew word that describes *a refuge* or *a place of shelter*. It depicts *protection, refuge*, and *shelter from dangers of all kinds and from storms and stormy situations*.

Friend, that is what God is to you — your *Refuge*! He is your protection and shelter from dangers of all kinds. Have you ever really stopped to think about that? Have you ever opened your mouth and declared out loud, "You are my Refuge, Father!" When you speak those words in faith into the atmosphere, His presence surrounds you and you begin to sense His protection encompassing you.

Not only is the Lord your Refuge, but He is also your *Fortress*. In Hebrew, the word "fortress" in Psalm 91:2 describes *a place of defense and protection*. It is the same word for *a castle, fortress*, or *stronghold*. It can even be translated as *a safe place of entanglement*. The use of this word indicates that you are so secure in Him that you are entangled in His protection and defense.

The verse goes on to say, "…In him will I trust" (Psalm 91:2). The phrase "will I trust" in Hebrew conveys the idea of *absolute confidence, absolute assurance*, and *absolute trust*. Wow! What a powerful declaration. Have you ever pressed pause on your life when everything seemed to be pressing against you, and said, "Lord, I completely trust You, and I'm absolutely confident You are protecting me and going to bring me through these situations." Although this goes against the grain of how you may feel or what you may see, it is God's cure for dealing with difficulties (*see* Romans 4:17).

The Bible Clearly Declares That God Is Our Refuge and Fortress

It is important to note that God's promise to be our Refuge and Fortress is not isolated to Psalm 91:2. On the contrary, it is a promise made throughout Scripture. Here are several passages confirming God's role as Refuge and Fortress in your life:

> **Deuteronomy 33:27** — The eternal God is thy *refuge*, and underneath are the everlasting arms….
>
> **2 Samuel 22:2** — …The Lord is my rock, and my *fortress*, and my deliverer.
>
> **Psalm 18:2** — The Lord is my rock, and my *fortress*, and my deliverer; my God, my strength, in whom I will trust; my buckler, and the horn of my salvation, and my high tower.
>
> **Psalm 27:5** — For in the time of trouble he shall hide me in his pavilion: in the secret of his tabernacle shall he hide me; he shall set me up upon a rock.

Psalm 31:20 — Thou shalt hide them in the secret of thy presence from the pride of man: thou shalt keep them secretly in a pavilion from the strife of tongues.

Psalm 46:1 — God is our *refuge* and strength, a very present help in trouble.

Psalm 62:6 — He only is my rock and my salvation: he is my defence; I shall not be moved.

Psalm 71:3 — Be thou my strong habitation, whereunto I may continually resort: thou hast given commandment to save me; for thou art my rock and my *fortress*.

Psalm 144:2 — My goodness, and my *fortress*; my high tower, and my deliverer; my shield, and he in whom I trust….

Proverbs 14:26 — In the fear of the Lord is strong confidence: and his children shall have a place of *refuge*.

Nahum 1:7 — The Lord is good, *a strong hold* in the day of trouble; and he knoweth them that trust in him.

In these passages, God is described twice as your *High Tower*. This means that He places you so high up that the enemy can't reach you. Sure, Satan and his minions will jump, stretch, and reach as high as they can to try to get you, but because the Lord is your High Tower and He places you high on a rock, the enemy cannot access you! In Christ, you are inaccessible to the enemy! When you're in the secret place of God's pavilion, not even the strife and gossip of people's tongues can reach and affect you.

Again, Psalm 91:2 in the original text says, "I will say TO the Lord, He is my refuge and my fortress: my God; in him will I trust." This means we are to take His promises to us, personalize them, and repeat them out loud back to Him. Friend, when you get the Word of God in your mouth and declare His promises back to Him — and speak them over yourself and those you love — you will activate His promises in your life. Indeed, He is your Never-Failing One and strong Refuge — so strong that no enemy can break through or break in to touch you!

STUDY QUESTIONS

> Study to shew thyself approved unto God, a workman that needeth not to be ashamed, rightly dividing the word of truth.
> — 2 Timothy 2:15

1. As you read through Psalm 91, what verse (or verses) really stand out to you? Which one (or ones) do you personally treasure most? Why does this verse (or these verses) mean so much to you?
2. The Bible says, "The eyes of the Lord search the whole earth in order to strengthen those whose hearts are fully committed to him…" (2 Chronicles 16:9 *NLT*). His desire to guard and protect you is all through Scripture. To strengthen your faith, take time to reflect on these promises, and jot down what the Holy Spirit is speaking to you through them.
   - Psalm 32:7; 119:114
   - Deuteronomy 33:27; Proverbs 18:10; Isaiah 25:4
   - Psalm 3:2-4; 5:12; 84:11; 125:1,2
   - Isaiah 41:10-14

PRACTICAL APPLICATION

> But be ye doers of the word, and not hearers only, deceiving your own selves.
> — James 1:22

1. "Abiding in the shadow of the Almighty" is all about *building relationship* with God. This includes life-giving practices like *daily prayer*, *reading and studying His Word*, and *spending time worshiping God and sitting in His presence*. Take a few moments and describe what building relationship with God looks like in *your* life. What kind of things do you do daily to stay close to Him?
2. If what you're doing to stay close to God isn't working, take time to pray and ask Him to show you what adjustments you need to make in your life to better connect with Him daily. What do you sense He wants you to SUBTRACT from your life? What does He want you to ADD?
3. When was the last time you cut out all the distractions and asked the Lord to really examine your life? There's no better time than the present to press pause on all your activity and pray as David prayed:

"Search me, O God, and know my heart; test my thoughts. Point out anything you find in me that makes you sad, and lead me along the path of everlasting life" (Psalm 139:23,24 *TLB*). As you are quiet and still before the Lord, listen for His voice. What is He showing you about *you*? What is He proud of? What changes do you feel He is asking you to make?

LESSON 4

TOPIC

Delivered From the Snare of the Fowler and the Noisome Pestilence

SCRIPTURES

1. **Psalm 91:1-3** — He that dwelleth in the secret place of the most High shall abide under the shadow of the Almighty. I will say of the Lord, He is my refuge and my fortress: my God; in him will I trust. Surely he shall deliver thee from the snare of the fowler, and from the noisome pestilence.
2. **Matthew 16:1** — The Pharisees also with the Sadducees came, and tempting....
3. **Matthew 19:3** — The Pharisees also came unto him, tempting him, and saying unto him, Is it lawful for a man to put away his wife for every cause?
4. **Matthew 22:15** — Then went the Pharisees, and took counsel how they might entangle him in his talk.
5. **Mark 12:13** — And they send unto him certain of the Pharisees and of the Herodians, to catch him in his words.
6. **Luke 11:53,54** — And as he said these things unto them, the scribes and the Pharisees began to urge him vehemently, and to provoke him to speak of many things: laying wait for him, and seeking to catch something out of his mouth....
7. **Psalm 140:1-5** — Deliver me, O Lord, from the evil man: preserve me from the violent man; which imagine mischiefs in their heart; continually are they gathered together for war. They have sharpened

their tongues like a serpent; adders' poison is under their lips. Selah. Keep me, O Lord, from the hands of the wicked; preserve me from the violent man; who have purposed to overthrow my goings. The proud have hid a snare for me, and cords; they have spread a net by the wayside; they have set gins for me. Selah.

8. **Psalm 140:1-5** (*NLT*) — O Lord, rescue me from evil people. Protect me from those who are violent, those who plot evil in their hearts and stir up trouble all day long. Their tongues sting like a snake; the venom of a viper drips from their lips. O Lord, keep me out of the hands of the wicked. Protect me from those who are violent, for they are plotting against me. The proud have set a trap to catch me; they have stretched out a net; they have placed traps all along the way.

9. **Psalm 35:7,8** — For without cause have they hid for me their net in a pit, which without cause they have digged for my soul. Let destruction come upon him at unawares; and let his net that he hath hid catch himself: into that very destruction let him fall.

10. **Proverbs 26:27** — Whoso diggeth a pit shall fall therein: and he that rolleth a stone, it will return upon him.

11. **Ecclesiastes 10:8** — He that diggeth a pit shall fall into it; and whoso breaketh an hedge, a serpent shall bite him.

12. **2 Thessalonians 1:6** — Seeing it is a righteous thing with God to recompense tribulation to them that trouble you.

GREEK WORDS

No Greek words were shown on the TV program.

SYNOPSIS

As we've noted in the first three lessons, Psalm 91 was written by Moses to the children of Israel after they had been delivered from slavery in Egypt and were making their way through the wilderness. It was during that time that they came face to face with wild animals, venomous snakes, and barbaric enemies that were bent on their destruction. Moses wrote Psalm 91 to refocus the Israelites on the promises of God's divine protection.

Like the children of Israel, if you're dealing with a spirit of fear because of all the attacks the enemy is bringing against you, it's time for you to grab hold of the protective promises of Psalm 91. If you will hide them in your heart and also put them in your mouth, you will activate God's promises and begin to see His power manifest in your life.

The emphasis of this lesson:

When you're abiding in the shadow of the Almighty and declaring His promises to Him and over your life, God will doubtlessly and with certainty snatch you away from the enemy's wicked plots and attacks and bring you into a place of safety.

You Are Called To 'Dwell in the Secret Place' Under the 'Shadow of the Almighty'

Psalm 91 opens with this powerful declaration: "He that dwelleth in the secret place of the most High shall abide under the shadow of the Almighty" (v. 1). We have seen that the word "dwelleth" in Hebrew means *to dwell, to lodge,* or *to take up residency.* It carries the idea of moving into a place and staying there permanently.

The place we are to move into and remain is called the "secret place." In Hebrew, this phrase depicts *an inner chamber, a place of concealment, a hiding place,* or *a secret compartment.* For believers, the "secret place" refers to being *in Christ.* The moment we are saved, we are placed in Christ, and He becomes our hiding place where we are deeply tucked away.

Now there are many people who are saved and have been placed in the secret place of Jesus, but because they are no longer "abiding under the shadow of the Almighty" (Psalm 91:1), they are unable to claim the protective promises of Psalm 91.

The words "shall abide" in Psalm 91:1 mean *to abide, dwell, lodge,* or *reside.* We are called to *abide* or *live* in the "shadow of the Almighty." If we're not abiding or dwelling in God's *shadow,* we cannot lay claim to His promises. The word "shadow" here describes *a shelter* or *a hiding place.* It also denotes *one who stays in step with the Lord.*

As we've noted, to abide in someone's shadow requires us to stay very close to him. When he moves, his shadow moves with him, so to stay in his shadow, we must stay in step with him. A person can be saved but not abiding closely to Jesus. These are Christians who have drifted away from devotion to Christ and are no longer passionately pursuing Him. In this distant, lukewarm condition — outside of the shadow of the Almighty — they cannot activate and experience God's protective promises.

Incidentally, the title "Almighty" in Psalm 91:1 is the Hebrew word *Shaddai*, which means *Great Provider* and *One Who Overpowers*. The use of the name *Shaddai* tells us that when we're walking in the shadow of the Almighty, we are *sheltered* and *protected* by God's supernatural presence.

God Will Most Assuredly Snatch Us Out of the Enemy's Snares

The psalmist goes on to say, "I will say of the Lord, He is my refuge and my fortress: my God; in him will I trust. Surely he shall deliver thee from the snare of the fowler, and from the noisome pestilence" (Psalm 91:2,3). Note the word "surely," which opens verse 3. It is a translation of the Hebrew term that means *but*, *certainly*, or *doubtless*, and it is a conjunction intended to make a dramatic point. Hence, we could translate this part of the verse to say, "Certainly, doubtlessly, without question he shall deliver thee…."

The words "shall deliver" in Hebrew mean *to deliver, plunder*, or *snatch away*. It carries the idea of one who is escaping or being defended. It is the picture of a person who is under attack and then suddenly snatched away to a place of safety. When we're abiding in the shadow of the Almighty and we're declaring His promises to Him and over our life, He will doubtlessly and with certainty snatch us away from the enemy's attacks.

Specifically, the psalm says the Lord will deliver us "from the snare of the fowler." In Hebrew, the words "from the snare" refer to *a bird trap*. In a figurative sense, this word describes *calamities, evil devices*, and *wicked plots* that are set to ensnare people. The second part — "of the fowler" — depicts *a fowler or trapper*. It is one who intentionally sets a trap to entangle and capture someone. Figuratively, it is used to picture a sinister plan to entangle a person.

Like a fowler, the devil and his demonic minions work through wicked men to attack God's people, and they operate stealthily so they can ensnare their victim by surprise. Many times we don't realize what they're doing — how they're secretly and clandestinely working to set a snare to try and catch us and take us down. The enemy will even change his methods so that he can't be detected. This "snare" is *a plan, plot, or scheme to hurt us* — or *even kill us.*

Thankfully, God promises that if you abide in the shadow of the Almighty, He will surely and most emphatically deliver you, snatching you out of the devil's snare and into a place of safety — thus short-circuiting the enemy's sinister plan to entangle you.

Jesus Was Snatched Out of the Sinister Schemes of the Religious Leaders

The Bible is filled with examples of wicked men working hand in hand with the enemy to ensnare God's people. Just think of all the times the Pharisees and the Sadducees tried to entangle Jesus and trip Him up in His own words. Again and again, they set up situations and asked Him questions publicly with the hopes of entrapping Him. Consider these passages from the gospels:

- **Matthew 16:1** says, "The Pharisees also with the Sadducees came, and tempting [Jesus]...."

- **Matthew 19:3** says, "The Pharisees also came unto him, tempting him, and saying unto him, Is it lawful for a man to put away his wife for every cause?" Here we see these religious leaders were trying to create a theological debate that would trip up Jesus and cause Him to answer in a way that was against Scripture.

- **Matthew 22:15** says, "Then went the Pharisees, and took counsel how they might entangle him in his talk."

- **Mark 12:13** states, "And they send unto him certain of the Pharisees and of the Herodians, to catch him in his words."

- **Luke 11:53 and 54** tell us, "And as he said these things unto them, the scribes and the Pharisees began to urge him vehemently, and to provoke him to speak of many things: laying wait for him, and seeking to catch something out of his mouth that they might accuse him."

Are you seeing the devilish pattern in these passages? The religious leaders repeatedly attempted to entangle and capture Jesus in their sinister schemes, but God was faithful to deliver Him out of every snare that was set before Him.

Esther and the Jews Were Delivered From Haman's Evil Plot

In addition to targeting individuals, the enemy also targets entire people groups, and the nation of Israel is a clear example. Right around the time when the Jewish people were coming out of their Babylonian captivity (586 - 516 BC) and under Persian rule, a man named Haman the Agagite rose to a position of great power. He despised the Jewish people and wanted desperately to wipe them from the earth.

Through a carefully woven scheme, Haman deceived the king of Persia into passing a law that called for the annihilation of the Jewish people. Moreover, there was one Jewish leader that Haman especially hated, and that was Mordecai, Esther's uncle. Mordecai had refused to bow and pay homage to Haman, so Haman had gallows built on which he planned to hang Mordecai.

But Haman's plot never saw the light of day. In fact, it totally backfired on him. When Queen Esther fearlessly went before the king and pled for her people to be saved, the king learned of Haman's sinister scheme to exterminate the Jews — which included his beloved queen. Enraged by Haman's evil plans, the king had Haman executed on the very gallows he had built to murder Mordecai. He then made Mordecai second in command and gave him the authority to write a new law that enabled the Jews to arm and defend themselves against anyone who attacked them (*see* Esther 8:1-11).

When the day of Israel's extermination finally came, the Bible says, "...The tables were turned and the Jews got the upper hand over those who hated them" (Esther 9:1 *NIV*). Instead of the Jewish people being destroyed, "The Jews struck down all their enemies with the sword, killing and destroying them..." (Esther 9:5 *NIV*). In the end, Haman and those who hated the Jews were ensnared in their own trap!

David Prayed To Be Delivered

Centuries before the story of Esther, a young man named David experienced his own set of overwhelming circumstances. Both before and after becoming king, David endured numerous attacks, which is why he regularly prayed for the Lord to deliver him. An example of his heart's cry to be rescued is found in Psalm 140:1-5, which says:

> Deliver me, O Lord, from the evil man: preserve me from the violent man; which imagine mischiefs in their heart; continually are they gathered together for war. They have sharpened their tongues like a serpent; adders' poison is under their lips. Selah. Keep me, O Lord, from the hands of the wicked; preserve me from the violent man; who have purposed to overthrow my goings. The proud have hid a snare for me, and cords; they have spread a net by the wayside; they have set gins for me. Selah.

Now here is this same passage — Psalm 140:1-5 — worded a little differently in the *New Living Translation*:

> O Lord, rescue me from evil people. Protect me from those who are violent, those who plot evil in their hearts and stir up trouble all day long. Their tongues sting like a snake; the venom of a viper drips from their lips. O Lord, keep me out of the hands of the wicked. Protect me from those who are violent, for they are plotting against me. The proud have set a trap to catch me; they have stretched out a net; they have placed traps all along the way.

Again and again, David prayed prayers like this to be delivered from the snare of the enemy, and God heard and answered his prayers! God is faithful, and what He did for David and the Jewish people, He will do for you. "For God does not show favoritism" (Romans 2:11 *NIV*).

The Wicked Will Be Ensnared in Their Own Traps

Knowing that our faith is built and strengthened by hearing the Word of God (*see* Romans 10:17), let's take a few moments to carefully read through some passages of Scripture that promise God's deliverance from the enemy's evil snares. As you reflect on these verses, pay attention to what is emphasized repeatedly:

> **Psalm 35:7,8** — For without cause have they hid for me their net in a pit, which without cause they have digged for my soul. Let destruction come upon him at unawares; and let his net that he hath hid catch himself: into that very destruction let him fall.

Proverbs 26:27 — Whoso diggeth a pit shall fall therein: and he that rolleth a stone, it will return upon him.

Ecclesiastes 10:8 — He that diggeth a pit shall fall into it; and whoso breaketh an hedge, a serpent shall bite him.

2 Thessalonians 1:6 — Seeing it is a righteous thing with God to recompense tribulation to them that trouble you.

Are you seeing the pattern in these verses? Now take a moment to read the *Renner Interpretive Version* (*RIV*) of Second Thessalonians 1:6, which contains the original Greek meaning:

God is always just and equitable, so you can be sure that He will repay the people who put you through all this misery! He will reimburse those who have afflicted you and see to it that they receive a full settlement of double trouble for the traumatic circumstances they put you through. God has a habit of being fair, so you can be certain that He will make sure everyone gets exactly what is deserved.

Friend, God promises again and again to watch over and take good care of you. In order to receive His protection, your part is to abide in the shadow of the Almighty. As you stay in step with *Shaddai* — *The Great Provider, The One Who Overpowers* — He "shall deliver thee from the snare of the fowler, and from the noisome pestilence" (Psalm 91:3).

God Will Deliver You From the 'Noisome Pestilence'

Interestingly, the word "noisome" in Hebrew describes *something deadly, greedy, destructive, mischievous, naughty,* or *perverse*. Figuratively, this word speaks of *the evil devices of people*. The truth is you and every other genuine believer around the world have had to or will have to deal with evil traps set by others. Nevertheless, if you continue to live in the shelter of the Almighty, you will be delivered from everything the enemy throws at you.

The Bible specifically says that God will deliver us from the noisome "pestilence." This is a translation of a Hebrew term that denotes *a pestilence, plague,* or *thorns*. In a figurative sense, it speaks of *sticky or thorny situations*. The word is related to a Hebrew word that means *to speak*, and thus, infers *sticky or thorny situations due to spoken words*. It can even describe *a great calamity that comes by surprise* or depict *a tragedy that hits suddenly and sweeps everything away in its destruction.* But regardless of what form the pestilence takes on, the Lord will protect His people who are abiding under His shadow. Thus, the deadly, ruinous, and destructive things have no power against us. They are defused because we're living and abiding in the shadow of the Almighty! Praise His mighty Name!

So what are you to "say *to* the Lord" in light of Psalm 91:3? With confidence, you can declare:

> *Surely, emphatically, and without a doubt, You will deliver me. You will snatch me out of calamities, evil devices, and wicked plots that are set to ensnare me. You will carry me into safety and deliver me from sinister attacks and deadly, destructive, perverse devices — even plagues — that people suddenly bring against me.*

In our next lesson, we will focus on Psalm 91:4 and discover what God means when He promises to "cover thee with his feathers, and under his wings shalt thou trust...."

STUDY QUESTIONS

> Study to shew thyself approved unto God, a workman that needeth not to be ashamed, rightly dividing the word of truth.
> — 2 Timothy 2:15

1. Remember how David talked about being delivered from the snare of the fowler and the deadly pestilence? Who else in Scripture was rescued from certain death and showed an entire empire that the God of Israel was real? (*See* Daniel 3 and 6 for the answer.)
2. The enemy's plot through Haman to exterminate the Jews is a classic example of the "snare of the fowler" described in Psalm 91:3. We know from Scripture that the sinister scheme backfired on Haman, and he was executed on the gallows that were built to hang Mordecai (*see* Esther 7:1-10). But how did God raise up and use Mordecai to flip the script on Satan? (*See* Esther 8:1-17.) What happened to the enemies of the Jews as a result of God's deliverance? (*See* Esther 9:1-17.)
3. How do these real-life stories in the book of Daniel and Esther encourage you and fan the flame of your faith to believe God to deliver you from the enemy's schemes?

PRACTICAL APPLICATION

> But be ye doers of the word, and not hearers only, deceiving your own selves.
> —James 1:22

1. Has God's rescue from trouble ever looked different than you thought, expected, or wanted? Briefly describe what took place and how you responded. What did it teach you about God and about yourself?
2. What is one sticky or thorny situation you've seen God miraculously deliver you from — or bring you through — in the past? Is there a present calamity or difficulty from which you need God to deliver you? If so, take time now to pray and invite Him into your circumstances. Ask Him to give you His *grace* to keep going until His deliverance fully comes.

LESSON 5

TOPIC

Covered With God's Feathers and Safe Under His Wings

SCRIPTURES

1. **Psalm 91:1-4** — He that dwelleth in the secret place of the most High shall abide under the shadow of the Almighty. I will say of the Lord, He is my refuge and my fortress: my God; in him will I trust. Surely he shall deliver thee from the snare of the fowler, and from the noisome pestilence. He shall cover thee with his feathers, and under his wings shalt thou trust: his truth shall be thy shield and buckler.

GREEK WORDS

No Greek words were shown on the TV program.

SYNOPSIS

Have you ever been tempted to be afraid? The children of Israel were — especially when they were making their way through the wilderness in the Sinai Peninsula. After being miraculously delivered from 400 years of slavery in Egypt, the Hebrew people were not accustomed to facing ferocious animals, poisonous snakes, and ungodly barbarians bent on their destruction. In fact, some of the Israelites were so afraid, they were seriously considering going back to Egypt.

It was during this critical time that Moses wrote Psalm 91, encouraging God's people to dwell in the secret place of the Most High and experience the divine protection of abiding under the shadow of the Almighty (*see* v. 1). Among the numerous promises of God's protection, Moses declared, "He shall cover thee with his feathers, and under his wings shalt thou trust…" (Psalm 91:4).

The emphasis of this lesson:

God's promise to cover us with His feathers means He will overshadow us with His presence and establish a supernatural hedge of protection around us. As we are securely entwined in Him, we can rest and place our trust in Him.

As a Believer in Christ, Jesus Is Your 'Secret Place'

Looking once more at Psalm 91:1, it says, "He that dwelleth in the secret place of the most High shall abide under the shadow of the Almighty." We've seen that the word "dwelleth" means *to dwell, to lodge*, or *to take up residency*. It describes a person who has moved into a place, put down roots, and become a permanent indweller.

The place he has permanently moved into is the "secret place," which in Hebrew describes *a private chamber, a place of secrecy, a hiding place,* or *a place of concealment*. For a born-again child of God, our secret place is being *in Christ*. The day we got saved, we were translated out of the kingdom of darkness and into the Kingdom of God and placed in Christ Jesus Himself (*see* Colossians 1:13). There's no place that is more secret and more secure than being in Him!

Jesus is the secret place of the Most High, and the Hebrew word for "Most High" is *Elyon*, which means *The One Who Is Supreme*. If you've made Jesus the Lord of your life, then you're eternally locked up in Him. His name is above every other name, and the day is coming when every knee will bow, and every tongue will confess and declare that Jesus Christ is Lord to the glory of God the Father (*see* Philippians 2:9-11). Scripture says, "God has made you complete in Christ. Christ is in charge of every ruler and authority" (Colossians 2:10 *GW*).

Psalm 91:1 goes on to say, "…[We] shall abide under the shadow of the Almighty." The word "shadow" describes *a shelter* or *a hiding place* and denotes *one who stays in step with the Lord*. When you're in God's shadow, you're in step with and hidden in Him.

Remaining in His 'Shadow' Is a Must

Now there are many people who've genuinely repented of their sin and received salvation in Christ, and while there was a time when they walked closely with the Lord, that is no longer the case. Over the years, as they've experienced various trials and troubles, they've drifted from their devotion to Jesus. Consequently, when they try to claim the promises of Psalm 91, they are unable to do so, and the reason is because these promises only work for those who *are abiding in the shadow of the Almighty*.

Remember, to stay in a person's shadow, you have to be pretty close to that person. This includes keeping a watchful eye on where he is and where he is going. If he moves, you must move with him. If you don't, you will no longer be in his shadow. To truly abide in this person's shelter, you must stay in step with him. Likewise, for you to stay in the shadow of the Almighty, you have to stay in step with the Lord, paying attention to when and where He is moving.

Again, the "shadow" of God is *a hiding place, a place of defense*, and *a place of protection* where all the promises of Psalm 91 are activated. He is the "Almighty" — the Hebrew word *Shaddai* — which means *Great Provider* and *One Who Overpowers*. When you're living in the shadow of the Almighty, you not only have divine protection, but you also have divine provision! The *Great Provider* is right there with you, and His power is working on your behalf to deliver you from everything evil that tries to come against you.

When You Voice God's Promises, His Delivering Power Is Activated in Your Life

Psalm 91:2 goes on to say, "I will say of the Lord, He is my refuge and my fortress: my God; in him will I trust." We've noted that in Hebrew, the opening of this verse actually says, "I will say TO the Lord...." This lets us know that the entire psalm is meant to be a *confession and declaration of faith*.

This means we need to fill our mouth with these verses. It's not enough to just think about, meditate on, and believe God's Word. Yes, these are all great practices and essential to our spiritual growth and well-being. But in order to experience His protective promises, we have to get His promises in our mouth and *speak* them aloud. When you voice your faith, the promises of God are activated and released into your life.

The Bible continues by saying, "Surely he shall deliver thee from the snare of the fowler, and from the noisome pestilence" (Psalm 91:3). The word "surely" in Hebrew means *certainly, emphatically,* or *doubtless*. It is a conjunction intended to make a dramatic point and the equivalent of saying, "Certainly, absolutely, emphatically He shall deliver thee from the snare of the fowler."

In Hebrew, the phrase "shall deliver" means *to deliver, plunder, or snatch away*. It carries the idea of one who is escaping or being defended — one who is snatched away out of danger and carried to a place of safety.

God Specializes In Snatching Us Out of Satan's Snares

Specifically, God will deliver us "from the snare of the fowler." The phrase "from the snare" is a translation of the Hebrew word for *a bird trap*. It was used figuratively to describe *calamities, evil devices, and wicked plots* that someone launched against others. The words "of the fowler" in Hebrew describe *a fowler* or *trapper*. It is one who intentionally sets a trap to entangle and capture something or someone. Used figuratively, it pictured a sinister plan to entangle a person.

In many ways, the devil and his demonic minions work through wicked men, acting like trappers. They attack God's people, often operating stealthily so they can ensnare their victims by surprise. The enemy will even change his methods so that he can remain undetected. The Pharisees and Sadducees did this repeatedly with the intent to ensnare Jesus. Haman did it to Mordecai and the Jews with the goal of exterminating the entire Jewish race.

The great news is that we have God's promise that those who set traps for us will fall into them themselves! This principle appears in multiple verses in the Bible, including passages like Proverbs 26:27 and Ecclesiastes 10:8. And Psalm 91:3 basically says, "Surely — emphatically, of a certainty, doubtless — He [God] will deliver you and snatch you out of danger, carrying you to a place of safety. He'll deliver you from the sinister plans which have been created against you...."

Deadly Situations Are No Match for the Almighty

The psalmist then adds that God will deliver us, "...from the noisome pestilence" (Psalm 91:3). We saw in our last lesson that the word "noisome" in Hebrew describes *something deadly*. It can also be translated as *greedy*, which makes sense because most attacks are based on greed. When someone is upset with you, it's often because you have something they want. Whether it's a possession or a position, they are greedy for what you have and will do whatever they can to get it.

Furthermore, the word "noisome" carries the idea of something *destructive*, *mischievous*, *naughty*, or *perverse*. Figuratively, it speaks of the evil devices people set up and use against you. Regardless of the exact manifestation, it is a "pestilence."

This word "pestilence" in Hebrew describes *pestilence*, *plagues*, or *thorns*, and it pictures *sticky or thorny situations*. What's interesting is that this word is closely related to the Hebrew word that means *to speak*, and it implies that the *thorny* or *sticky situations* have come about as a result of *words* that someone has spoken. If you stop to think about it, most problems are created by words that people speak. Thankfully, God promises that if you abide in the shadow of the Almighty, He will surely and most emphatically deliver you, snatching you out of the devil's snare and into a place of safety.

When we personalize Psalm 91:3, we have a confession of faith that declares:

> *You will deliver me from the snare of the fowler; You will deliver me from noisome pestilence.*

God Will Cover Us
With His Feathers, Under His Wings

When we come to Psalm 91:4, we find the next protective promise, which says, "He shall cover thee with his feathers, and under his wings shalt thou trust: his truth shall be thy shield and buckler." Like all the verses before it, verse 4 is also filled with many important words.

First, note the word "cover." It is a translation of a Hebrew word that means *to fence in, hedge in, cover, overshadow, protect, screen,* or *shut in.* In some cases, it meant *to enweave or entwine,* and it pictured *complete concealment, entwinement, protection, and security.* The use of this term here tells us that God will fence us in and establish a supernatural hedge around us. Indeed, He will cover us, overshadow us, protect us, and entwine us in His presence to such an extent that we are completely protected and secure.

How will God cover us? Scripture says, "…with his feathers, and under his wings…" (Psalm 91:4). The word "feathers" in Hebrew refers to *pinions* or *feathers,* and the word "wings" denotes *wings used of birds* as well as *wings of cherubim or seraphim,* which is extremely significant. It can also describe *garments.*

Between the words *feathers* and *wings* is the word "under" — a translation of the Hebrew word meaning *below* or *underneath.* What's interesting here is that the original Hebrew text fully states, "You will take refuge and confidently trust underneath his wings." This implies that we are *hiding behind God's back, behind His power,* or *behind His reputation.* This is an impenetrable place of peace and safety.

Three Uses of the Word 'Wings'

The word *wings* in Hebrew is very important. First, it was used to picture *the wings of a bird* — especially a mother bird that put her wings around her baby birds to protect them because they cannot protect themselves.

Second, the word *wings* was used figuratively to describe *wrapping garments around someone.* In the context of Psalm 91, it pictures God wrapping His arms like garments around those who walk closely with Him and live in His shadow. It's as if He's wrapping us in His garments or putting us under His royal robe to conceal us and protect us. That's what happens when you live in the shadow of the Almighty.

The third important use of the Hebrew word for *wings* relates to the Ark of the Covenant. The Ark had a thick lid made of pure gold with two cherubim on its top. Each cherubim faced the center and had wings that were extended toward each other and over the center of the Ark's cover. It was between those wings that the presence of God rested (*see* exodus 25:19-22). Therefore, when this verse says, "…Under his wings shalt thou trust" (Psalm 91:4), it is inferring that we are to remain close to the presence of God. To stay under His wings meant abiding in His manifest presence, which hovered under the wings of the two angels.

When you're dwelling under the shadow of the Almighty, you're in God's presence, and in His presence, there is supernatural protection, safety, provision, deliverance, and shelter. The verse goes on to say that "…under his wings shalt thou trust…" (Psalm 91:4). The words "shalt thou" describe *our* part, which is to make it our endeavor to live in the presence of God — under His wings — and to continually trust Him.

Again, Psalm 91:4 says, "He shall cover thee with his feathers, and under his wings shalt thou trust…." When we personalize this passage, we have a confession of faith that declares:

> *You cover me with Your feathers. You put me safely under Your wings….*

In our next lesson, we will examine the remainder of Psalm 91:4, which states, "…His truth shall be thy shield and buckler," along with the promise of Psalm 91:5, which declares, "Thou shalt not be afraid for the terror by night; nor for the arrow that flieth by day."

STUDY QUESTIONS

Study to shew thyself approved unto God, a workman that needeth not to be ashamed, rightly dividing the word of truth.
— 2 Timothy 2:15

1. If you have ever struggled to believe that God wants to — and is able to — deliver you, carefully read what David wrote in Psalm 34. Note how many times he said that God will deliver you, and note what He promises to deliver you from.

2. Psalm 91:3 says, "Surely he [God] shall deliver thee from the snare of the fowler, and from the noisome pestilence." To really grab hold

of God's willingness to rescue you, take some time to look up these passages in a few different Bible versions. Write down the scriptures in the translation that speaks to you most deeply and commit these promises to memory:
- 1 Corinthians 10:13
- 2 Corinthians 1:10
- 2 Timothy 4:18
- 2 Peter 2:9
- Psalm 116:8
- Isaiah 46:4

PRACTICAL APPLICATION

> But be ye doers of the word, and not hearers only, deceiving your own selves.
> —James 1:22

1. God wants you to abide under the covering of His protection and trust Him to always keep you safe. Be honest: Do you find it difficult to trust God for His protection? If so, why? What are you afraid will happen? Which is more of a struggle: believing God CAN protect you or believing that He WILL protect you? As you are open and honest with God, He will deliver you from all your fears (*see* Psalm 34:4).

2. When you look back over your life, where can you see the divine protection of God covering your life? How about the lives of your family? Don't rush. Take your time and invite the Holy Spirit to bring to your memory every saving situation through which God has brought you. The more you can count, the stronger your faith will grow that He will do it again!

3. Carefully meditate on these powerful promises of God's protection:
The Lord God is my Strength, my personal bravery, and my invincible army; He makes my feet like hinds' feet and will make me to walk [not to stand still in terror, but to walk] and make [spiritual] progress upon my high places [of trouble, suffering, or responsibility]! (Habakkuk 3:19 *AMPC*)

God guards you from every evil, he guards your very life. He guards you when you leave and when you return, he guards you now, he guards you always. (Psalm 121:7,8 *MSG*)

…He [God] Himself has said, I will not in any way fail you nor give you up nor leave you without support. [I will] not, [I will] not, [I will] not in any degree leave you helpless nor forsake nor let [you] down (relax My hold on you)! [Assuredly not!] So we take comfort and are encouraged and confidently and boldly say, The Lord is my Helper; I will not be seized with alarm [I will not fear or dread or be terrified]. What can man do to me? (Hebrews 13:5,6 *AMPC*)

What is the Holy Spirit speaking to you through these amazing scriptures?

LESSON 6

TOPIC

His Truth, Your Shield and Buckler — No Fear of the Terror by Night or the Arrow That Flieth by Day

SCRIPTURES

1. **Psalm 91:1-5** — He that dwelleth in the secret place of the most High shall abide under the shadow of the Almighty. I will say of the Lord, He is my refuge and my fortress: my God; in him will I trust. Surely he shall deliver thee from the snare of the fowler, and from the noisome pestilence. He shall cover thee with his feathers, and under his wings shalt thou trust: his truth shall be thy shield and buckler. Thou shalt not be afraid for the terror by night; nor for the arrow that flieth by day.
2. **Psalm 3:5** — I laid me down and slept; I awaked; for the Lord sustained me.
3. **Psalm 4:8** — I will both lay me down in peace, and sleep: for thou, Lord, only makest me dwell in safety.
4. **Psalm 56:3** — What time I am afraid, I will trust in thee.

5. **Psalm 127:2** — It is vain for you to rise up early, to sit up late, to eat the bread of sorrows: for so he giveth his beloved sleep.
6. **Proverbs 3:24** — When thou liest down, thou shalt not be afraid: yea, thou shalt lie down, and thy sleep shall be sweet.

GREEK WORDS

No Greek words were shown on the TV program.

SYNOPSIS

Living under the shadow of the Almighty is the safest place in the world to live! He is your Refuge and Fortress as Psalm 91:2 proclaims. He is also your *Guardian God*! As the psalmist says, "God's your Guardian, right at your side to protect you.... God guards you from every evil, he guards your very life. He guards you when you leave and when you return, he guards you now, he guards you always" (Psalm 121:5,7,8 *MSG*). Friend, you have no reason to fear the terrors of the night nor the attacks that take place during the day. God is on your side and at your side, as you abide by His side in the shadow of the Almighty.

The emphasis of this lesson:

God's Word is absolute truth, and we are to allow it to become hooked in our heart and soul as a shield that securely covers our life. The more His Word fills us, the more it shields us and protects us. He doesn't want us to fear surprise attacks that come during the day or the terrors of the night. We can sleep in peace because He makes us dwell in safety.

A Review of Psalm 91:1-3

History documents that the nation of Israel was enslaved by the Egyptians for more than 400 years, but God delivered them from bondage through the leadership of Moses. After their deliverance from Egypt, they began to experience things they weren't accustomed to — things like venomous snakes, ferocious wild beasts, and surprise attacks from enemies in the land. As fear began to infiltrate their hearts and minds, Moses wrote the protective promises of Psalm 91, which begins in verse 1 by saying:

> **He that dwelleth in the secret place of the most High shall abide under the shadow of the Almighty.**

Here again is a quick overview of the key words in this passage:

"Dwelleth" — In Hebrew, this word means *to dwell, to lodge,* or *to take up residency.* It depicts *one who moves into a place and stays there permanently.*

"Secret Place" — In Hebrew, this describes *an inner chamber, a place of concealment, a hiding place,* or *a place of secrecy.* It denotes *the most secret compartment.* As believers, Jesus is our *secret place.* The moment we surrendered our life to God, He placed us *in Christ,* and we took up permanent residency in Him. There is no deeper, more secure place in God than to be in Christ!

"Most High" — In Hebrew, this is the word *Elyon,* which means *The One Who Is Supreme.* That is who Jesus is — *The One Who Is Supreme.* Paul wrote about this truth in Colossians 2:10 where he said that Christ "…is the head of all principality and power." If you're saved, you're *in Christ,* and you are complete in Him, *The One Who Is Supreme* above all.

"Shadow" — In Hebrew, this describes *a shelter* or *a hiding place* and carries the idea of *one who stays in step with the Lord.* To walk in someone's shadow, you have to be very close to them. If they move, you must move with them, and you must move in the same direction at the same pace. Otherwise, you will soon be out of their shadow.

"Almighty" — In Hebrew, this is the word *Shaddai,* which means *Great Provider* and *One Who Overpowers.*

Every promise in Psalm 91 belongs to those who are abiding in the shadow of the Almighty. This is a picture of us drawing near to the Lord, clinging to Him, and staying so close to Him that we're living in step with His shadow. Christians who drift away from Jesus and move out of His shadow also move out from under God's protective promises.

When we come to Psalm 91:2, it says, "I will say of the Lord, He is my refuge and my fortress: my God; in him will I trust." We've noted that in the original Hebrew text, the opening of this verse says, "I will say TO the Lord," which tells us clearly that Psalm 91 is a *confession* — or *declaration* — of faith. Thus, we are to take these verses, personalize them, and repeat them back to the Lord.

The psalmist continued in Psalm 91:3: "Surely he shall deliver thee from the snare of the fowler, and from the noisome pestilence." Essentially, when we insert the Hebrew meaning of this verse, we could personalize it to say:

> *Surely, emphatically, and without a doubt, You, God, will deliver me. You will snatch me out of calamities, evil devices, and wicked plots that are set to ensnare me. You will carry me into safety and deliver me from sinister attacks and deadly, destructive, perverse devices — even plagues — that others bring against me.*

God Himself Is Our Covering

As we move to Psalm 91:4, we discover yet another protective promise, which says, "He shall cover thee with his feathers, and under his wings shalt thou trust: his truth shall be thy shield and buckler." We learned in our last lesson that the word "cover" is a Hebrew word that means *to fence in, hedge in, cover, overshadow, protect, screen,* or *shut in*. In some cases, it means *to enweave or entwine* and pictures *complete concealment, entwinement, protection, and security*.

The use of this word lets us know that God desires to fence us in and hedge us in on all sides. Indeed, He will cover us, overshadow us, protect us, and entwine us in His presence to such an extent that we are completely protected and secure. And the Scripture says He does this, "…with his feathers, and under his wings…" (Psalm 91:4).

The word "under" is a translation of the Hebrew word meaning *below* or *underneath*. What's interesting here is that the original Hebrew text fully states, "You will take refuge and confidently trust underneath his wings." Wow! Essentially, this means that when we're "covered with God's feathers and under His wings," we are *hiding behind God's back, behind His power*, or *behind His reputation*. God Himself has stepped out in front of us to protect us!

We Are Under His 'Wings'

Pay close attention to the word "wings" in Psalm 91:4 because it's important. In Hebrew, the word "wings" denotes three specific things: *wings used of birds, wings of cherubim or seraphim,* and *flowing garments that wrap around someone*.

When used to represent *wings of a bird*, they especially illustrate a mother bird that put her wings around her little chicks to protect them because they cannot protect themselves. Hence, God protects us like a mother bird protects her defenseless babies.

The word *wings* was also used figuratively to describe *wrapping garments around someone*. In the context of Psalm 91, it pictures God wrapping His arms around us like garments as we walk closely with Him and live in His shadow. It's as if He's wrapping us in His velvety, royal robe to conceal us and protect us. That's what happens when you live in the shadow of the Almighty.

The third important use of the Hebrew word for *wings* is linked to the Ark of the Covenant. The Ark had an ornate lid made of pure gold with two cherubim on its top. The two angels faced one another and had wings that were extended toward and over the center of the Ark. The Bible says that between and under those wings the presence of God hovered and rested (*see* Exodus 25:19-22).

What does all this mean to you? Well, when Scripture says, "…Under his wings shalt thou trust" (Psalm 91:4), it is implying that you are to abide in God's manifest presence. When you're dwelling under the shadow of the Almighty, you're living in God's presence, and in His presence, there is supernatural protection, safety, provision, deliverance, and shelter. The words "shalt thou trust" describe our part, which is to make every effort to live in the presence of God — under His wings of protection — and to continually trust in Him.

The Truth Is Our 'Shield and Buckler'

Psalm 91:4 concludes by saying, "…His truth shall be thy shield and buckler." The word "truth" in this verse is a Hebrew word describing *absolute truth*; *unchanging truth*; *faithful truth*; *stable truth*; or *trustworthy truth*. As long as you view the Word of God as *absolute, unchanging truth* and you live by it, it will be a "shield and a buckler" for you.

The word "shield" in Hebrew denotes *a hook* or *a covering shield*. The use of this word lets us know that we are to let the Word of God — *His absolute truth* — become hooked in our heart and soul. The more God's truth is hooked in our lives, the greater a covering shield of defense it will be.

The truth also functions as a "buckler" in our life. In Hebrew, this word describes *a small shield* or *a traveling companion*. Hence, as a small shield, it protects us, and the fact that it operates like a travel companion means it is *a weapon* to accompany those who abide in the shadow of the Almighty.

Are you seeing all the many reasons there are for you to live and to abide as close to God as you can? When you abide and take up residence in the shadow of the Almighty, God's promise of divine protection is yours! God's Word serves as a shield to you and all who trust and believe it, to those who claim it and boldly confess it by faith. It will provide protection for you along every road you travel in life.

Again, the promise of Psalm 91:4 states, "He shall cover thee with his feathers, and under his wings shalt thou trust: his truth shall be thy shield and buckler." When we personalize this passage, we have a confession of faith that declares:

> *You cover me with Your feathers. You put me safely under Your wings. Your truth is my shield and my buckler.*

God Promises Peace and Safety During the Night

Continuing our journey through Psalm 91, verse 5 says, "Thou shalt not be afraid for the terror by night; nor for the arrow that flieth by day." The first remarkable aspect of this verse is that "thou shalt not be afraid." The Hebrew meaning of "afraid" is *to dread* or *to fear*. As you abide in the shadow of the Almighty, you will not dread or fear the "…terror by night; nor for the arrow that flieth by day" (Psalm 91:5).

The word "terror" in Hebrew describes *a dreadful fear* or *terror*, and the words "by night" literally mean *by night*. Remember, when Israel left Egypt and was in the wilderness, they experienced many challenges, which included the frightening shrieks and screams of animals in the night. In fact, nighttime in the wilderness was likely a time when everyone was super sensitive to every sound around them. Indeed, the Israelites were confronted with real terror. Yet through Moses, God said, "Thou shalt not be afraid for the terror by night; nor for the arrow that flieth by day" (Psalm 91:5).

This promise of divine peace and protection from enemy attacks in the night is repeated all through Scripture. In fact, God even guarantees us sleep when we lie down at night. Consider these promises in Psalms and Proverbs:

> **Psalm 3:5** — I laid me down and slept; I awaked; for the Lord sustained me.
>
> **Psalm 4:8** — I will both lay me down in peace, and sleep: for thou, Lord, only makest me dwell in safety.
>
> **Psalm 127:2** — It is vain for you to rise up early, to sit up late, to eat the bread of sorrows: for so he giveth his beloved sleep.
>
> **Proverbs 3:24** — When thou liest down, thou shalt not be afraid: yea, thou shalt lie down, and thy sleep shall be sweet.

Few things are more valuable than regular sleep at night. Researchers say that just going 24 hours without sleep can cause impaired vision, hearing, and hand-eye coordination — not to mention irritability, reduced memory function, and impaired decision-making. Clearly, we need quality sleep on a regular basis, and God knows it. If you struggle to get a good night's rest, commit these verses to memory and speak them to the Lord and over you and your family every night. As David declared, you too can declare: "What time I am afraid, I will trust in thee" (Psalm 56:3).

You Are Also Shielded From the Effects of Daytime Attacks

In addition to living fear-free from the terror of night, God says we should also not be afraid of "…the arrow that flieth by day" (Psalm 91:5). In Hebrew, the word "arrow" means *dart* or *that which pierces*. It can also be used figuratively of the lion's teeth. The phrase "that flieth" in Hebrew describes *something that flies* and refers to both *speed* and *surprise*. It can also mean *to faint, to flee away*, or *to weary*, which describes the effect of this arrow.

The *arrow that flieth* is "by day," which literally means *in the daytime*. This is God's guarantee of protection against any attack that comes during the day. The "arrow that flieth by day" refers to outright, visible attacks from the enemy that take place in plain sight. What this verse is telling us is that regardless of the kind of attack or the time of attack — day or night — God's supernatural hedge of protection will surround you if you are abiding in the shadow of the Almighty.

Remember, He is your Shelter, your Hiding Place, and your Refuge. There is no safer place on the planet than the secret place of the Most High, so don't abandon your place of abiding! Stay in step with the Lord. Spend time with Him, cling to Him, hold tightly to His Word, live under His wings in His presence. When you're in His shadow, His divine protection overshadows your life.

Again, God's promise in Psalm 91:5 says, "Thou shalt not be afraid for the terror by night; nor for the arrow that flieth by day" (Psalm 91:5). When we personalize this verse, we have a confession of faith that declares:

I will not be afraid of the terror by night. I will not be afraid of the arrow that flies by day.

Friend, you have no reason to fear the destruction during the day or any terror that takes place in the night. You are safe and secure as you abide in the shadow of the Almighty! In our next lesson, we will examine what it means to not be afraid of "…the pestilence that walketh in darkness; nor for the destruction that wasteth at noonday" (Psalm 91:6).

STUDY QUESTIONS

Study to shew thyself approved unto God, a workman that needeth not to be ashamed, rightly dividing the word of truth.
— 2 Timothy 2:15

1. In Scripture, the word "wings" denotes three specific things: wings used of birds, wings of angels, and flowing garments that wrap around a person. Of these three aspects, which one is most meaningful to you personally? Why is that?
2. Essentially, Psalm 91:4 says that if you view the Word of God as *absolute, unchanging truth* and you live by it, it will be a "shield and a buckler" for you. Be honest: How do you view God's Word? What does God say about His Word in Second Timothy 3:16,17 and Second Peter 1:20,21 that is vital for us to always keep in mind?

PRACTICAL APPLICATION

But be ye doers of the word, and not hearers only, deceiving your own selves.
— James 1:22

1. Are you having difficulty falling asleep and staying asleep at night? If so, take a few moments to pray, "Lord, is there anything I'm doing that is disturbing my ability to sleep? Am I listening to or watching things that are keeping me awake? Am I eating or drinking something that's hindering my body from winding down and resting? Please show me anything I need to change, Lord, and give me the strength to change it. In Jesus' name."
2. God knows you need rest and has promised to give it to you! Take time to reflect on and commit to memory God's promises to give you sleep in Psalm 3:5; 4:8; 127:2; and Proverbs 3:24. Now go one step further and personalize each verse, declaring them to the Lord and over yourself nightly. You will be amazed at the difference your confession of faith has on your sleep!
3. Have you surrendered your life to Christ and made Him your Savior and Lord? If you haven't, you can! All it takes is a humble heart and a willingness to come to God and say, "Father, I believe Jesus is Your Son whom You sent to pay the price for all my sins, which I ask You to forgive me of now. Jesus, You are Lord, and I invite You into my life to be *my* Lord. Thank You for loving me and wanting to be in relationship with me. In Your Name. Amen!"

LESSON 7

TOPIC

I Will Not Fear the Pestilence That Walks in Darkness or the Destruction That Wastes at Noonday

SCRIPTURES

1. **Psalm 91:1-6** — He that dwelleth in the secret place of the most High shall abide under the shadow of the Almighty. I will say of the Lord, He is my refuge and my fortress: my God; in him will I trust. Surely he shall deliver thee from the snare of the fowler, and from the noisome pestilence. He shall cover thee with his feathers, and under his wings shalt thou trust: his truth shall be thy shield and buckler.

Thou shalt not be afraid for the terror by night; nor for the arrow that flieth by day; nor for the pestilence that walketh in darkness; nor for the destruction that wasteth at noonday.

2. **Psalm 3:5** — I laid me down and slept; I awaked; for the Lord sustained me.
3. **Psalm 4:8** — I will both lay me down in peace, and sleep: for thou, Lord, only makest me dwell in safety.
4. **Proverbs 3:24** — When thou liest down, thou shalt not be afraid: yea, thou shalt lie down, and thy sleep shall be sweet.

GREEK WORDS

No Greek words were shown on the TV program.

SYNOPSIS

Have you heard the old saying, "Sticks and stones can break my bones, but words will never hurt me"? We know that statement is far from true. The fact is words can be devastating — especially words of slander and gossip. Few things can do more damage faster than the human tongue. The good news is that those who abide in the shadow of the Almighty are promised protection from all such pestilence. We find this promise not only in Psalm 91:6 but also in Psalm 31:20 (*NLT*), where David declares, "You [God] hide them in the shelter of your presence, safe from those who conspire against them. You shelter them in your presence, far from accusing tongues." Do you want protection from the poisonous words of people? You'll find it in the shelter of God's presence!

The emphasis of this lesson:

When you abide in the shadow of the Almighty, you don't have to be afraid of any plague or any thorny situations that result from slanderous words others have spoken. Likewise, you are not to fear any form of destruction that seeks to ruin your life. Why? Because God is your shield.

Psalm 91 Was Written by Moses To the Children of Israel

The Bible records that the children of Israel had been in slavery in Egypt for more than 400 years, and to a great degree, they became like city folk who were only acclimated to living in the "big city." When they left Egypt and were on the way to the Promised Land, they found themselves in the middle of the wilderness where they encountered things that they had never faced before.

Foreign enemies, ferocious animals, venomous snakes, and scorpions were not something they were used to, and nighttime was especially hard because they were hearing all kinds of eerie sounds from animals in the wild. Confronted with fear like never before, Moses penned and proclaimed the protective promises of God in Psalm 91, which begins in verse 1 by saying:

> **He that dwelleth in the secret place of the most High shall abide under the shadow of the Almighty.**

'Dwelling in the Secret Place of the Most-High' Means…

The word "dwelleth" in Hebrew means *to dwell, to lodge*, or *to take up residency*. It carries the idea of moving into a place and staying there permanently. Rather than being a guest that periodically visits God's presence, this describes one that is a permanent indweller in the *secret place*.

In Hebrew, the words "secret place" depict *an inner chamber, a place of concealment, a hiding place*, or *a secret compartment*. For believers, this refers to us being placed *in Christ* the moment we are saved. He becomes our hiding place where we are deeply tucked away in the Most High. There is no safer, more secure place than being in Christ!

The words "Most High" in Hebrew is *Elyon*, which means *The Supreme One* who has authority over all. This is consistent with the description of Jesus in Colossians 2:10, which says, "And ye are complete in him, which is the head of all principality and power."

To Activate God's Promises, We Must 'Abide' in His Presence

Again, to claim the promises of Psalm 91, we need to *abide in the shadow of the Almighty*. The words "shall abide" in Psalm 91:1 mean *to abide, dwell, lodge*, or *reside*. We are called to *abide* or *live* in the "shadow of the

Almighty." If we're not abiding or dwelling in God's *shadow*, we cannot lay claim to His promises.

The word "shadow" here describes *a shelter* or *a hiding place*. It also denotes *one who stays in step with the Lord*. To abide in someone's shadow involves staying very close to that person. His shadow moves every time he moves, so to stay in his shadow, we must stay in step with him. Just as you can be in the same room with someone but far from him or her, a person can be saved and in Christ but not abiding closely to Him.

Although the reasons vary, there are some Christians who drift away from their passionate pursuit of Jesus. Little by little, they grow distant and become lukewarm, and as a result, they are no longer in the shadow of the Almighty, leaving them unable to activate and lay claim to His protective promises.

Psalm 91 Is Our Declaration of Faith

When we come to Psalm 91:2, it says, "I will say of the Lord, He is my refuge and my fortress: my God; in him will I trust." We learned that the original Greek text of this verse begins by saying, "I will say TO the Lord," which tells us clearly that Psalm 91 is meant to be *a declaration of faith*. These promises are to be in your mouth, not just in your mind. It's not enough just to *think* about them — we must also declare these promises aloud to God and speak them over our life in order to activate them.

The psalmist continues in Psalm 91:3, saying, "Surely he shall deliver thee from the snare of the fowler, and from the noisome pestilence." The word "surely" would better be translated *emphatically, with all certainty*, and *without a doubt*. And the phrase "shall deliver" in Hebrew means *to snatch out of danger and carry to a place of safety*.

When we insert the Hebrew meaning into this verse, we see that it can be translated, "God will most assuredly deliver you and snatch you from the enemy's deadly traps and bring you into a place of safety. He will even deliver you from the sinister schemes crafted to capture and kill you."

Valuing God's Word as Absolute Truth Makes It Our 'Shield and Buckler'

In Psalm 91:4, we see the next protective promise, which says, "He shall cover thee with his feathers, and under his wings shalt thou trust: his truth shall be thy shield and buckler." We saw in previous lessons that God's promise to cover us with His feathers and wings is His guarantee of supernatural protection, safety, provision, deliverance, and shelter.

We also learned that the word "truth" describes *absolute truth*; *unchanging truth*; *faithful truth*; *stable truth*; or *trustworthy truth*. According to this verse, if you view and value the Word of God as absolute truth, it will become a "shield and a buckler" for you. The word "shield" here has two meanings in Hebrew: it describes both a *hook* and *a shield*. This lets us know that God's Word needs to be *hooked* into our heart and soul, and when His truth becomes hooked in us, it takes on the form of a *shield* that covers and protects our life.

God's truth also functions as a "buckler" for us, which in Hebrew is a word that describes *a small, round shield* or *a traveling companion*. The use of this word informs us that when we value Scripture as absolute truth, it begins to function as a shield as well as a weapon that travels with us everywhere we go in life.

Protection and Sleep at Night Are God's Guarantee

The next promise in Psalm 91 deals with sudden attacks. The Bible declares, "Thou shalt not be afraid for the terror by night; nor for the arrow that flieth by day" (Psalm 91:5). The Hebrew meaning of "afraid" is *to dread* or *to fear*. As you abide in the shadow of the Almighty, you have no need to dread or fear the "…terror by night; nor for the arrow that flieth by day" (Psalm 91:5).

We saw that the word "terror" describes *a dreadful fear* or *terror*, and the words "by night" literally mean *during the night*. Bear in mind that the people of Israel were in the wilderness for the first time in more than 400 years, and while they initially may have thought that nighttime would be quiet and restful, it wasn't. Instead, they heard all kinds of frightening shrieks and screams.

Think about when you're alone at night in a strange place — or even in your own home. It's as if someone turned up the volume and you can hear every creak and thump throughout the house. This experience was magnified for the people of Israel in the wilderness. Even so, Moses told them, "Thou shalt not be afraid for the terror by night; nor for the arrow that flieth by day" (Psalm 91:5).

The same promise is available to you. When you're living in the shadow of the Almighty and you're safe and secure under His wings, supernatural peace and protection are yours. As a matter of fact, God also guarantees you sleep. Take another look at these promises from Psalms and Proverbs:

Psalm 3:5 — I laid me down and slept; I awaked; for the Lord sustained me.

Psalm 4:8 — I will both lay me down in peace, and sleep: for thou, Lord, only makest me dwell in safety.

Psalm 127:2 — It is vain for you to rise up early, to sit up late, to eat the bread of sorrows: for so he giveth his beloved sleep.

Proverbs 3:24 — When thou liest down, thou shalt not be afraid: yea, thou shalt lie down, and thy sleep shall be sweet.

Friend, if you're faced with fear at night, begin to speak these promises out loud over you and your family every night. Instead of popping a bunch of pills to go to sleep, make the Word of God your medication of choice! Simply open your mouth and begin to declare by faith:

I will lie down and sleep, and I will wake up again because God will sustain me.

I will lie down in peace and sleep because the Lord makes me dwell in safety.

God gives me, His beloved, the gift of sleep.

Therefore, when I lie down, I will not be afraid; I will lie down, and my sleep will be sweet!

These are God's promises to you as you abide in the shadow of the Almighty! He wants you to live a fear-free existence — even during the night.

God Also Diffuses Daytime Attacks

God also said we are not to be afraid of "...the arrow that flieth by day" (Psalm 91:5). In Hebrew, the word "arrow" means *dart* or *that which pierces*, and the phrase "that flieth" describes *something that flies* and expresses the idea of both *speed* and *surprise*. Furthermore, the words "by day" literally mean *in the daytime.*

Therefore, when we read about the "arrow that flieth by day," it refers to *outright, visible attacks from the enemy that take place in plain sight.* In this passage, God guarantees protection against any such attack — day or night. If you are in the secret place of Jesus Christ, abiding in the presence of God, His supernatural hedge of protection will surround you and keep you safe, regardless of the time or type of attack that comes.

Remember, He is your Shelter, your Hiding Place, and your Refuge. There is no safer place on the planet than the secret place of the Most High, so don't abandon the place of abiding! Stay in step with the Lord. Spend time with Him, cling to Him, hold tightly to His Word, and live under His wings in His presence. When you're in His shadow, His divine protection overshadows your life.

Again, Psalm 91:5 in its entirety says, "Thou shalt not be afraid for the terror by night; nor for the arrow that flieth by day." When we personalize this verse, we have a confession of faith that states:

I will not be afraid of the terror by night. I will not be afraid of the arrow that flies by day.

People's Words Cannot Plague Your Life

As we continue our journey through Psalm 91, the next protective promise in verse 6 is closely connected with verse 5. Verse 6 says, "Nor for the pestilence that walketh in darkness; nor for the destruction that wasteth at noonday." Here, God is telling us that as we stay close to Him, we will not have to be afraid of *pestilence.*

In Hebrew, the word "pestilence" describes *pestilence, a plague,* or *thorns.* Figuratively, it speaks of *sticky or thorny situations.* Interestingly, this word is related to a Hebrew word that means *to speak,* and thus, it infers *sticky or thorny situations due to spoken words.* No doubt, we can cause great damage with the words we speak.

If you think about it, it's the careless words of people who spread rumors and slanderous allegations that lead to deep hurt and broken relationships. Nevertheless, according to Psalm 91:6, if you abide in the shadow of the Almighty, you don't have to be afraid of sticky situations because of what others have said or alleged.

To be clear, this passage specifies that the pestilence "walketh in darkness." The word "walketh" in Hebrew literally means *accompanies* darkness. We could even say this word *exercises itself* in darkness or *spreads about* in darkness.

This is a perfect picture of how gossip works. It is very clandestine and moves stealthily in darkness. People don't talk openly about things they wish to gossip about, and the reason they try to keep things secret is because they know they shouldn't be talking about others. In fact, it's no surprise that the Greek word for "gossip" means *to whisper*. The reason people are whispering is because they know they're not supposed to be saying what they're saying.

A good rule to follow when it comes to talking about others is if you can't say it out loud in front of everyone, then you shouldn't say it at all. If we fail to follow this rule, we create sticky or thorny situations that "walketh in darkness." The word "darkness" here describes *darkness, obscurity,* or *gloom*. Hence, it's something stealthy. Again, if you're abiding in the shadow of the Almighty, you don't need to be afraid of that.

'Destruction' Cannot Lay Waste to You

Psalm 91:6 goes on to say that we don't need to be afraid of "…the destruction that wasteth at noonday." In Hebrew, the word "destruction" refers to *anything that destroys*. The word wasteth is also important. It means *to lay waste, to violently lay waste*, or *to completely ruin*, and this happens at "noonday," which means *in the very middle of the day*. Hence, it is an attack that is carried out in plain view.

So the intention of this destructive attack is to lay waste completely and totally ruin everything in your life. However, if you're abiding in the shadow of the Almighty, neither the enemy nor evil people can succeed in their efforts.

Again, Psalm 91:6 in its entirety says, "Nor for the pestilence that walketh in darkness; nor for the destruction that wasteth at noonday." When we personalize this passage, we have a confession of faith that declares:

> *I will not fear pestilence that walks in darkness. I will not fear destruction that wastes at noonday.*

In our next lesson, we will examine what is meant when the Bible says, "No evil befall thee, neither shall any plague come nigh thy dwelling."

STUDY QUESTIONS

> **Study to shew thyself approved unto God, a workman that needeth not to be ashamed, rightly dividing the word of truth.**
> — 2 Timothy 2:15

1. *Gossip* is a classic example of the "pestilence that walketh in darkness" (Psalm 91:6). It operates in secrecy and moves stealthily in darkness. What does God have to say in His Word about gossip, slander, and those who are "talebearers"? Take a look at these verses for the answer:
   - Leviticus 19:16
   - Proverbs 18:8 and 26:22-26
   - Proverbs 16:27,28
   - Proverbs 11:13; 17:9; and 20:19
   - Psalm 101:5

2. What sobering statement does Jesus make in Matthew 12:35-37 about careless (or idle) words? What does this say to you personally about your own words?

3. Thankfully, through the power of the Holy Spirit, we can learn to master our mouth and use our words for good rather than evil. According to Psalm 34:12,13; First Peter 3:10; and Proverbs 13:3; 21:23, what are the rewards of restraining the tongue? And what do Ephesians 4:29-32 and Colossians 4:6 say our speech should be like?

PRACTICAL APPLICATION

> **But be ye doers of the word, and not hearers only, deceiving your own selves.**
> — James 1:22

1. The word "pestilence" can describe *sticky or thorny situations due to spoken words*. Have you ever been the victim of gossip or slanderous words that were spoken to hurt you and damage your reputation? If so, briefly share what happened. How is God redeeming the situation and turning things around for your good?

2. Have you ever gossiped or said something harsh or derogatory against someone else and it really hurt them? If so, what took place? Have you prayed and asked God to forgive you? Have you gone to the person

you wronged, apologized, and asked for their forgiveness? If not, take time now to humble yourself before God and deal with the situation. Ask Him for the strength, the words, and the timing to go to the person you hurt and make things right.

LESSON 8

TOPIC

No Evil Shall Befall Thee, Neither Shall Any Plague Come Nigh Thy Dwelling

SCRIPTURES

1. **Psalm 91:1-10** — He that dwelleth in the secret place of the most High shall abide under the shadow of the Almighty. I will say of the Lord, He is my refuge and my fortress: my God; in him will I trust. Surely he shall deliver thee from the snare of the fowler, and from the noisome pestilence. He shall cover thee with his feathers, and under his wings shalt thou trust: his truth shall be thy shield and buckler. Thou shalt not be afraid for the terror by night; nor for the arrow that flieth by day; nor for the pestilence that walketh in darkness; nor for the destruction that wasteth at noonday. A thousand shall fall at thy side, and ten thousand at thy right hand; but it shall not come nigh thee. Only with thine eyes shalt thou behold and see the reward of the wicked. Because thou hast made the Lord, which is my refuge, even the Most High, thy habitation; There shall no evil befall thee, neither shall any plague come nigh thy dwelling.

2. **Romans 10:9,10** — That if thou shalt confess with thy mouth the Lord Jesus, and shalt believe in thine heart that God hath raised him from the dead, thou shalt be saved. For with the heart man believeth unto righteousness; and with the mouth confession is made unto salvation.

GREEK WORDS

No Greek words were shown on the TV program.

SYNOPSIS

In today's world, we are well aware of the presence of evil and of the existence of plagues. But just because evil exists and sickness abounds, it doesn't mean they can automatically invade your life. God said, "Because thou hast made the Lord, which is my refuge, even the Most High, thy habitation; there shall no evil befall thee, neither shall any plague come nigh thy dwelling" (Psalm 91:9,10). As you abide in God's presence and hold tightly to His Word, He becomes a supernatural shield of protection against everything the enemy tries to throw at you! What a mighty God we serve!

The emphasis of this lesson:

When people are dropping all around you, whatever plague or calamity that's causing it will emphatically not come near you or have any effect on you. Only with your eyes will you see and ponder the reward of the wicked. This is God's promise to you for making the choice to make Him your habitation.

A Quick Review of Our Anchor Verse

The children of Israel had been living in Egypt for more than 400 years, and even though those years were marked by the hardship of slavery, they weren't faced with the unusual challenges of living in the wilderness. Once the Israelites left Egypt, they encountered foreign enemies, ferocious beasts, poisonous snakes, and all kinds of wild animals that stalked through the night. As fear began to beat on the door of their hearts, God used Moses to pen the protective promises of Psalm 91, which starts off in verse 1 by saying:

> **He that dwelleth in the secret place of the most High shall abide under the shadow of the Almighty.**

We've seen that the word "dwelleth" in Hebrew means *to dwell, to lodge*, or *to take up residency*. It depicts a person who has moved into a place and decided he is going to live there forever. For believers, this describes being placed *in Christ* the moment we were saved. He is our "secret place of the Most High." Again, the title "Most High" is the Hebrew word *Elyon* — meaning *The Supreme One*. Indeed, no one is superior to Jesus, and there is no place safer and more secure than being in Him!

The second part of the verse says that we "…shall abide under the shadow of the Almighty" (Psalm 91:1). The word "shadow" here describes *a shelter* or *a hiding place*. It also denotes *one who stays in step with the Lord*, which makes sense because to stay in the Lord's shadow, we need to live right alongside Him. When He moves, we must move with Him, and when He stops, we stop. The implication here is that we are walking intimately close to Christ, clinging to His presence. And in His presence is fullness of joy (*see* Psalm 16:11).

Are You Putting These Truths in Your Mouth?

Hopefully it is sinking in — that to lay claim and activate the protective promises of Psalm 91, you have to abide in the shadow of the Almighty. That is, you must live in God's presence, in close relationship with Him. Additionally, you need to put His promises in your mouth. As we've noted, the real power of faith is not released until words of faith are spoken from our mouth.

Psalm 91:2 says, "I will say of the Lord, He is my refuge and my fortress: my God; in him will I trust." Keep in mind that the original Hebrew text of this verse actually says, "I will say TO the Lord…." This wording tells us that this psalm was written to be a confession and declaration of faith. We are to put these verses in our mouth and repeat them out loud to God and over our life.

When we personalize **Psalm 91:2**, we have a confession of faith that states:

> *I will say to You, Lord: You are my refuge; You are my fortress; You are my God. I trust in You.*

Psalm 91:3 says, "Surely he shall deliver thee from the snare of the fowler, and from the noisome pestilence." When we personalize this verse, we have a confession of faith that declares:

> *You will deliver me from the snare of the fowler; You will deliver me from noisome pestilence.*

Psalm 91:4 says, "He shall cover thee with his feathers, and under his wings shalt thou trust: his truth shall be thy shield and buckler." When we personalize this verse, we have a confession of faith that states:

You cover me with Your feathers; You put me safely under Your wings. Your truth is my shield and buckler.

Psalm 91:5 says, "Thou shalt not be afraid for the terror by night; nor for the arrow that flieth by day." When we personalize this passage, we have a confession of faith that declares:

I will not be afraid of the terror by night; I will not be afraid of the arrow that flies by day.

Psalm 91:6 says, "Nor for the pestilence that walketh in darkness; nor for the destruction that wasteth at noonday." When we personalize this verse, we have a confession of faith that proclaims:

I will not fear pestilence that walks in darkness; I will not fear destruction that wastes at noonday.

Again, these are not passages that you're to just ponder in your mind and believe in silence. Rather, you are to say them out loud to the Lord. What God said to Jeremiah He is still saying to us: "…He who has My word, let him speak My word faithfully…" (Jeremiah 23:28 *NKJV*).

People May Fall All Around You, but It Will Not Come Near You

When we come to Psalm 91:7, we read God's promise, "A thousand shall fall at thy side, and ten thousand at thy right hand; but it shall not come nigh thee." This passage is simply packed with meaning.

First, notice the word "a thousand." In Hebrew, this is *a thousand* and refers to *a large number*. The phrase "shall fall" means *to fall, to lie*, or *to fall by accident*. It can also mean *to fall by violent death* or *to suffer as a result of falling*. "At thy side" in Hebrew means *beside you* or *at your nearby side*. Thus, when the Bible says, "A thousand shall fall at thy side," it is saying, "A large number of people shall fall right beside you and shall suffer, and some will fall by a violent death."

Next, we see the words "ten thousand at thy right hand." The Hebrew meaning of "ten thousand" is *ten thousand*, and it indicates *a multitude or myriad of people*. "At thy right hand" is a translation of a Hebrew word meaning *at your right hand*, as the left hand is already referred to. Thus, people shall fall on both sides.

The Protective Promises of Psalm 91 | 67

Amazingly, even though a large number of people have fallen on your left side and an even larger multitude has fallen on your right, "...It shall not come nigh thee" (Psalm 91:7). The words "shall not" in Hebrew mean *emphatically not*, and "come nigh" means *to approach* or *come near*. So when people are dropping like flies around you — left and right — whatever is causing it will emphatically not come near you or have any effect on you. When we take this entire verse and personalize it, we have a declaration of faith that says:

> *A thousand will fall at my side, and ten thousand at my right hand, but it will not come nigh me.*

You Will Only Be a Spectator of the Fate the Befalls the Wicked

Psalm 91:8 continues the thought started in verse 7, stating, "Only with thine eyes shalt thou behold and see the reward of the wicked." The word "only" in Hebrew means *only* or *at the least*, which means only your eyes will come in contact with the demise of the wicked.

This brings us to the phrase "shalt thou behold," which in Hebrew means *to behold, consider, contemplate, look, regard*, or *see*. And the word "see" means *to see with your eyes*. In context, this verse is essentially saying, "It's a guarantee that you're never going to taste of or experience the reward of the wicked; you're only going to see it and contemplate their fate with your eyes."

In Hebrew, the word "reward" describes *a full recompense and retribution*, and the word "wicked" describes *those who do what is criminal, wicked, or wrong; those who are guilty of doing what is morally wrong*. The reason you are not going to experience what the wicked experience is because you are living in the shadow of the Almighty. When you're walking that closely to Jesus and abiding in His presence, you will have a driving desire to do what's right — not what's wrong.

When we take Psalm 91:8 and personalize it, we have a declaration of faith that says:

> *Only with my eyes will I behold and see the reward of the wicked.*

A Personal Decision Is Required

Psalm 91:9 and 10 goes on to say, "Because thou hast made the Lord, which is my refuge, even the Most High, thy habitation; There shall no evil befall thee, neither shall any plague come nigh thy dwelling."

Notice verse 9 begins with the word "because." This word points to the *result* of living in the shadow of the Almighty. The verse then says, "Thou has made," which is a phrase indicating that we have willfully chosen to take action. Specifically, we must choose "to make the Lord our refuge and our habitation." No one can make this choice for us. Each of us must decide to make Jesus the Lord of our life and come into the secret place.

Now, look closely at that word "Lord." In both the New Testament and Old Testament Septuagint, which is the Greek version, the word "Lord" is *Kurios*, and it describes *the one with ultimate authority in every realm — visible and invisible*. No one has a higher status than the *Lord*, which is the term used to describe Jesus. Again, you must make a decision to submit to His ultimate authority. Yes, He is our Savior who has redeemed our soul from sin and Satan's power, but have you made Him *Lord* of your life? Are you living in submission to Him as the highest authority in your life?

Believe It in Your *Heart* Confess It With Your *Mouth*

Romans 10:9 says, "That if thou shalt confess with thy mouth the Lord Jesus, and shalt believe in thine heart that God hath raised him from the dead, thou shalt be saved." The word "Lord" in this verse is the same Greek word used in Psalm 91:9 — the word *Kurios*, which means *the Supreme Master, the one with ultimate authority in every realm — visible and invisible*. To confess with your mouth that Jesus is Lord is to surrender your life to Him in total obedience.

The next verse says, "For with the heart man believeth unto righteousness; and with the mouth confession is made unto salvation" (Romans 10:10). Here again, we find the principle that faith doesn't just think — it *speaks*. Yes, the Bible says with the heart man believes unto righteousness, but it's with the mouth that confession is made unto salvation. Once we believe God's Word in our heart, we need to put it in our mouth and speak it out.

The reason this is so important is because words of faith are released through the words of our mouth. Your voice represents your authority. When you say, "Jesus is the Lord of my life," you're throwing open the door for Him to exercise His ultimate authority in your life.

'No Evil Shall Befall Thee'

Returning to Psalm 91, verse 10 says, "There shall no evil befall thee, neither shall any plague come nigh thy dwelling." The word "evil" here is a Hebrew word that describes *affliction* or *anything bad*. It denotes *calamity, distress, evil, injury,* or *misery*. It can also refer to *unhappiness* or *sadness*. When you're living in the shadow of the Almighty, none of these things will "befall thee." The word "befall" in Hebrew means *to befall, to encounter,* or *to meet*.

If you're living in the shadow of the Almighty, you're not going to encounter or run into any of these evil things. Why? Because His shadow is a hiding place — a place of safety and joy. There's no sadness or sorrow in the supernatural shelter of God's presence.

The Bible goes on to say, "…Neither shall any plague come nigh thy dwelling." The words "any plague" in Hebrew describe *an attack*, *plague*, or *strike*, and while it can be a spiritual or mental attack, this word here especially refers to *a physical sickness* or *a physical wound*. Again, when you're abiding in the shadow of the Almighty, no attack, no plague, and no strike of any kind will *come nigh thy dwelling*.

The Hebrew word for "come nigh" means *to approach or come near*, and "thy dwelling" depicts *a tent* or *the place where one lives*. Essentially, it is *a place of dwelling and residence*. If your residence or dwelling place is in the shadow of the Almighty, no attack or plague will even approach you or come near you. Sickness and disease cannot dwell in the shadow of the Almighty. It is the safest place on the planet for you to live!

Once more, Psalm 91:9 and 10 says, "Because thou hast made the Lord, which is my refuge, even the Most High, thy habitation; There shall no evil befall thee, neither shall any plague come nigh thy dwelling." When we personalize these verses, we have a declaration of faith that proclaims:

> *I have made the Lord my refuge. I have made the Most High my habitation. No evil will befall me; no plague will come nigh my dwelling.*

In our next lesson, we will take a close look at the amazing role of angels and how God has commissioned them to guard and protect us in all our ways.

STUDY QUESTIONS

> Study to shew thyself approved unto God, a workman that needeth not to be ashamed, rightly dividing the word of truth.
> — 2 Timothy 2:15

1. Take a few moments to slowly read Psalm 91:7 and 8 — along with its meaning in Hebrew. Then do the same with Psalm 91:9 and 10. What is the Holy Spirit showing you about appropriating these particular promises in light of all that is going on in the world today?
2. As frustrating as it is to see the wicked seemingly prospering in everything they do, their day of reckoning is coming. What does the Bible say about the "payday" that is on the way for the wicked? Consider what the Holy Spirit spoke through these passages:
   - Psalm 37:2,9,10,13,14,17,20,28,34-38
   - Psalm 55:23; Proverbs 5:22,23
   - Psalm 11:5,6; Proverbs 14:12; Philippians 3:18,19
   - Psalm 92:7; Revelation 21:8
3. Are you struggling to trust that the wicked will indeed get what's coming to them? You're not alone. The writer of Psalm 73 felt the same way and was on the verge of walking away from God's presence. But when he humbled himself and drew close to God, something extraordinary happened. Carefully read this psalm and see what God showed this man about himself and what awaits the wicked. In what specific ways did God change his heart?

PRACTICAL APPLICATION

> But be ye doers of the word, and not hearers only, deceiving your own selves.
> — James 1:22

1. If you have repented of your sins and received the gift of salvation through Jesus, He has become your personal Savior. But is He also

your *Lord*? Have you truly surrendered your life to Him, and are you living in submission to Him daily — obeying His Word in both the big and little things?
2. In what areas of your life do you find it easier to submit and obey the Lord's instructions? In what areas is it most difficult? Why do you think that is the case? Take a moment to pray and get God's input. Say, "Lord, why am I resistant to You in these areas? Is it pride? Or am I afraid of something? Please reveal to me what's going on inside me and help me obey You, in Jesus' name."

LESSON 9

TOPIC

He Shall Give His Angels Charge Over Thee To Keep Thee and Bear Thee Up in Their Hands

SCRIPTURES

1. **Psalm 91:1-12** — He that dwelleth in the secret place of the most High shall abide under the shadow of the Almighty. I will say of the Lord, He is my refuge and my fortress: my God; in him will I trust. Surely he shall deliver thee from the snare of the fowler, and from the noisome pestilence. He shall cover thee with his feathers, and under his wings shalt thou trust: his truth shall be thy shield and buckler. Thou shalt not be afraid for the terror by night; nor for the arrow that flieth by day; nor for the pestilence that walketh in darkness; nor for the destruction that wasteth at noonday. A thousand shall fall at thy side, and ten thousand at thy right hand; but it shall not come nigh thee. Only with thine eyes shalt thou behold and see the reward of the wicked. Because thou hast made the Lord, which is my refuge, even the most High, thy habitation; There shall no evil befall thee, neither shall any plague come nigh thy dwelling. For he shall give his angels charge over thee, to keep thee in all thy ways. They shall bear thee up in their hands, lest thou dash thy foot against a stone.

2. **Hebrews 1:14** — Are they not all ministering spirits, sent forth to minister for them who shall be heirs of salvation?
3. **Matthew 18:10** — Take heed that ye despise not one of these little ones; for I say unto you, That in heaven their angels do always behold the face of my Father which is in heaven.
4. **Psalm 34:7** — The angel of the Lord encampeth round about them that fear him, and delivereth them.

GREEK WORDS

No Greek words were shown on the TV program.

SYNOPSIS

Writing under the anointing of the Holy Spirit, the apostle Paul prophesied what the world would be like in the last of the last days. With great urgency, he said, "This know also, that in the last days perilous times shall come" (2 Timothy 3:1). Without question, the days we are living in are perilous and filled with challenges of all kinds that surround us on all sides. If there was ever a time we needed God's supernatural protection, it's now. Thankfully, God has provided us with the protective promises of Psalm 91, and they are just as powerful today as the day they were penned!

The emphasis of this lesson:

God's promises to you in Psalm 91 also include the guarantee of angelic protection. Certain angels have been explicitly assigned to you — and your children and grandchildren — to watch over, protect, and preserve you in your ways and on every road of life God leads you.

Why Do We Have Psalm 91?

As we've noted, Psalm 91 was written by Moses to the children of Israel at the time of their great departure from the enslaving power of the Egyptians. As they made their trek throughout the wilderness, they came face to face with things they had not encountered for four centuries. Because they had basically lived as city dwellers all those years in captivity, they were quite shaken when they began to encounter brute beasts like lions and jackals, not to mention venomous snakes and scorpions.

As the terror of the night and the sudden attacks at noonday began to take their toll, Moses heard from God and wrote the words of Psalm 91, which begin by saying, "He that dwelleth in the secret place of the most High shall abide under the shadow of the Almighty" (v. 1). The key to understanding and activating the promises of this Psalm is found in this anchor verse. With that in mind, let's run through the meaning of the key words once more.

> The **"secret place"** describes *a secret chamber, a place of privacy, a hiding place,* or *a place of concealment.* As believers, it describes us being placed *in Christ.* The moment we're saved, we are tucked away deeply in Him — He is the secret place of the Most High, and there is no safer place than inside of Jesus.
>
> The words **"Most High"** in Hebrew is *Elyon,* and it means *The One Who Is Supreme.* This is a direct reference to Jesus Himself. Because you are tucked away deeply in Christ, the Bible says, "…You are complete in Him, who is the head of all principality and power" (Colossians 2:10 *NKJV*).
>
> Psalm 91:1 goes on to say that we "…shall abide under the shadow of the Almighty." The word **"shadow"** describes *a shelter* or *a hiding place. Thus, it is a place where you can hide and find protection.* Equally important, it denotes *one who stays in step with the Lord.*
>
> Lastly, the word **"Almighty"** in Hebrew is the word *Shaddai,* which means *Great Provider* and *One Who Overpowers.* Indeed, our God provides everything we need and overpowers and overcomes everyone that is ranged against us. Friend, when you're dwelling in the shadow of the Almighty, His shadow of protection, provision, and overcoming power falls on you, and all that He is and has is made available to you.

Remember, for you to abide in His shadow, you have to walk very close to Him and stay in step with Him. Just as a person's shadow only extends so far, so does God's. If He moves and you don't move with Him, you will quickly be out of His shadow. Hence, inferred in this promise is that you have to stay in step with the Lord for you to be in His shadow.

Are You 'Saying It' to the Lord?

In addition to understanding Psalm 91:1, it is also vital that you grasp the meaning of verse 2, which says, "I will say of the Lord, He is my refuge and my fortress: my God; in him will I trust." We've noted that the original Hebrew text here says, "I will say TO the Lord." This lets us know up front that this entire chapter is not something we're to just think about and believe internally. We're also supposed to say it out loud. These verses are a confession and declaration of faith. Here again is Psalm 91:2-8:

> **I will say of the Lord, He is my refuge and my fortress: my God; in him will I trust.**
>
> **Surely he shall deliver thee from the snare of the fowler, and from the noisome pestilence.**
>
> **He shall cover thee with his feathers, and under his wings shalt thou trust: his truth shall be thy shield and buckler.**
>
> **Thou shalt not be afraid for the terror by night; nor for the arrow that flieth by day;**
>
> **Nor for the pestilence that walketh in darkness; nor for the destruction that wasteth at noonday.**
>
> **A thousand shall fall at thy side, and ten thousand at thy right hand; but it shall not come nigh thee.**
>
> **Only with thine eyes shalt thou behold and see the reward of the wicked.**

These promises from God are simply fabulous! To help you practice "saying it to the Lord," slowly reread each verse aloud, and after you read each one, personalize it and speak your declaration of faith to the Lord.

Make the Lord Your 'Habitation' and No Evil Will 'Befall' You

When we come to Psalm 91:9 and 10, the psalmist shifts our attention back to the importance of abiding in God's presence. Beginning in verse 9, it says, "Because thou hast made the Lord, which is my refuge, even the most High, thy habitation." Notice the word "habitation." In Hebrew, it means *dwelling*, *habitation*, or *place of residence*. The use of this term paints yet another picture of us dwelling in and making the shadow of the Almighty our residence.

The phrase "my refuge" also reinforces the idea of living in God's presence. In Hebrew, it describes *a refuge* or *shelter*. Moreover, the Hebrew word for "Most High" is *Elyon*, which means *The One Who Is Supreme*. When we insert all this meaning into the verse, it says, "Because you have made the Lord, which is your refuge and shelter, even The One Who Is Supreme your habitation or place of residency."

Verse 10 then declares the result of our decision. It says, "There shall no evil befall thee, neither shall any plague come nigh thy dwelling" (Psalm 91:10). The word "evil" here is a translation of the Hebrew term for *affliction*. It denotes *something bad*, *a calamity*, or *a distress*. It is *evil* or *something causing injury*, *misery*, *unhappiness*, or *sadness*. Again, if you've made the Lord's presence your habitation, no evil will befall you.

This word "befall" in Hebrew means *to befall*, *to encounter*, or *to meet*. If you've made the decision to abide in the shadow of the Almighty, you are not going to encounter or meet up with calamity, misery, or injury. It won't befall you — neither will "any plague," which in Hebrew describes *an attack*, *plague*, or *strike*. It specifically denotes *a physical sickness* or *a physical wound*.

Here we have the promise that if you're living in the shadow of the Almighty, you're not going to be stricken with some kind of physical or mental sickness. Why? Because God's presence is filled with goodness, and no sickness or evil of any kind can dwell there. It must leave! Indeed, no plague will "come nigh your dwelling."

The phrase "come nigh" means *to approach* or *to come near*, and the word "dwelling" is the Hebrew word for *a tent*. It refers to your physical body, which, like a tent, is the temporary place where you live. So no plague is going to come near or approach you — your body or your physical residence. Why? Again, the reason is your physical residence is in the shadow of the Almighty, and sickness cannot exist there. Clearly, this is the best place on earth for you to live.

God Has Assigned Angels To Guard You!

One of the greatest promises in Psalm 91 appears in verses 11 and 12. Here, the Bible declares, "For he shall give his angels charge over thee, to keep thee in all thy ways. They shall bear thee up in their hands, lest thou dash thy foot against a stone." As you might expect, there are several key words in these verses.

First, notice the word "angels." In both Hebrew and Greek, it is the word for *angels* or *divine messengers*. The words "give…charge" are also important. This is a translation of the Hebrew word meaning *to appoint, charge, command,* or *ordain*. It indicates *giving an explicit assignment or responsibility*, such as a charge that was given to a servant to do a task without negligence. In such a moment, the master would describe the mission explicitly to the servant so that it couldn't be misunderstood.

According to Psalm 91:11, the Lord has given an explicit assignment to angels "…to keep thee in all thy ways." In Hebrew, the phrase "to keep thee" means *to keep; to guard; to preserve;* or *to watch*. It is from a root word meaning *to hedge about*, which means the angels literally surround those who are dwelling in the shadow of the Most High! This principle of angelic protection is confirmed in both the Old and New Testaments.

Regarding angels, Hebrews 1:14 says, "Are they not all ministering spirits, sent forth to minister for them who shall be heirs of salvation?" Isn't that amazing! Angels are dispatched to minister to every single person who is inheriting salvation.

Jesus Himself said in Matthew 18:10, "Take heed that ye despise not one of these little ones; for I say unto you, That in heaven their angels do always behold the face of my Father which is in heaven." Did you catch that? Jesus said every child has angels assigned to them — most likely from birth — and those guardian angels not only protect and assist these children, but they also stand in the very presence of God.

Even the Psalms talk about the work of angels. For example, Psalm 34:7 says, "The angel of the Lord encampeth round about them that fear him, and delivereth them." Here we see that angels bring delivering power to those who reverently fear and worship God. Again, these angels who have been assigned to assist us who are inheriting salvation are charged "to keep us in all our ways."

The words "in all" in Psalm 91:11 in Hebrew mean *all, altogether, in all manner,* or *in all ways*. The phrase "thy ways" in both Hebrew and Greek indicates *in all your roads or courses of life*. Hence, on every road of life that you take, angels have been charged by God to protect you, preserve you, and guard you.

What Exactly Do Angels Do?

Psalm 91:12 says, "They shall bear thee up in their hands, lest thou dash thy foot against a stone." Note the phrase "they shall bear thee up." It is a translation of the Hebrew word meaning *to advance, bring forth, carry,* or *lift up*. Moreover, the word "hands" in Hebrew refers to *the palm of the hands*. What's interesting here is that angels are not only assigned to hold us up in their hands but also *bring us forth and cause us to advance*.

Now, as you are being carried in the palm of the hands of angels, the angel's job is to keep you from *dashing your foot against a stone*. The phrase "dash thy foot" in Hebrew means *to dash, gore, hurt, stumble, strike,* or *stub*. And the words "against a stone" denote *an encumbrance, like a stone, that has been set in your way*. Hence, this is a picture of someone who has fallen into some kind of calamity or distress.

Psalm 91:11 and 12 reveal that God extends protection and care to His people through angels. He commands them to explicitly keep us and bear us up in the palm of their hands — even helping us advance and move forward in life. Angels are to accompany, defend, and preserve those who dwell in the shadow of the Almighty. If necessary, angels will even turn your steps in another direction and reroute you to avoid danger. They've been charged to carefully watch over all the interests of anyone who abides in the shadow of the Almighty.

Again, Psalm 91:11 and 12 state, "For he shall give his angels charge over thee, to keep thee in all thy ways. They shall bear thee up in their hands, lest thou dash thy foot against a stone." When we personalize these verses so we can repeat them to the Lord as Psalm 91:2 instructs us, we have a confession and declaration of faith that says:

> *You give Your angels charge over me to keep me in all my ways. Your angels bear me up in their hands, lest I dash my foot against a stone.*

In our final lesson, we will examine the remainder of Psalm 91 and discover what God means when he says, "I'll give you victory over all the works of the enemy, satisfy you with long life, and show you My salvation!"

STUDY QUESTIONS

> Study to shew thyself approved unto God, a workman that needeth not to be ashamed, rightly dividing the word of truth.
> — 2 Timothy 2:15

1. Prior to this lesson, what did you know about *angels*? Did you know that God has specifically assigned them the responsibility to watch over, protect, and preserve you (*see* Psalm 91:11,12)? Were you aware of Jesus' sobering words in Matthew 18:10 about the work of guardian angels with our children? How do these verses give you hope?

2. In Job 1:10, God gives us an eye-opening look into the invisible realm of the spirit. What does this verse reveal about God's care of Job and his family? What does this say to you about God's care for *you* and *your family* — especially considering His promise in Acts 10:34,35; Romans 2:11 and 10:12?

3. The fact is that angels have been — and continue to be — on assignment since the beginning of creation. Consider these few examples of how supernatural beings have materialized in the natural world to accompany, assist, and divinely protect everyday people. In each passage, note *who* was being helped and *what the angel (or angels) did*:

   - Genesis 19:1-29
   - Genesis 32:1,2
   - Exodus 14:19,20
   - Numbers 22:21-35
   - Judges 13:2-24
   - Daniel 6:21,22
   - Matthew 1:18-25; 2:13-16
   - Luke 1:5-20
   - Luke 1:26-39
   - Luke 22:39-43
   - John 20:10-14
   - Acts 12:6-10

PRACTICAL APPLICATION

> But be ye doers of the word, and not hearers only, deceiving your own selves.
> — James 1:22

1. Isn't it amazing that angels have been dispatched to minister to and assist every single person who is inheriting salvation (*see* Hebrews 1:14). This means that in addition to angels helping you, they're also helping your friends and family members who presently aren't saved but will be

saved in the days ahead. How does this news encourage your faith and motivate you to pray for your unsaved loved ones?

2. The psalmist said, "Bless the Lord, you His angels, Who excel in strength, who do His word, Heeding the voice of His word" (Psalm 103:20 *NKJV*). The word "heeding" here carries the idea of *observing* and *listening for*. The angels listen for the voice of God's Word and then do His Word. Can you see the connection between this passage and Psalm 91:2? Are you beginning to grasp the vital importance of *speaking* God's Word over yourself and your family?

LESSON 10

TOPIC

God Says: I'll Give You Victory Over All the Works of the Enemy, Satisfy You With Long Life, and Show You My Salvation!

SCRIPTURES

1. **Psalm 91:1-16** — He that dwelleth in the secret place of the most High shall abide under the shadow of the Almighty. I will say of the Lord, He is my refuge and my fortress: my God; in him will I trust. Surely he shall deliver thee from the snare of the fowler, and from the noisome pestilence. He shall cover thee with his feathers, and under his wings shalt thou trust: his truth shall be thy shield and buckler. Thou shalt not be afraid for the terror by night; nor for the arrow that flieth by day; nor for the pestilence that walketh in darkness; nor for the destruction that wasteth at noonday. A thousand shall fall at thy side, and ten thousand at thy right hand; but it shall not come nigh thee. Only with thine eyes shalt thou behold and see the reward of the wicked. Because thou hast made the Lord, which is my refuge, even the most High, thy habitation; There shall no evil befall thee, neither shall any plague come nigh thy dwelling. For he shall give his angels charge over thee, to keep thee in all thy ways. They shall bear thee up

in their hands, lest thou dash thy foot against a stone. Thou shalt tread upon the lion and adder: the young lion and the dragon shalt thou trample under feet. Because he hath set his love upon me, therefore will I deliver him: I will set him on high, because he hath known my name. He shall call upon me, and I will answer him: I will be with him in trouble; I will deliver him, and honour him. With long life will I satisfy him, and shew him my salvation.

2. **Luke 10:19** — Behold, I give you power to tread on serpents and scorpions, and over all the power of the enemy: and nothing shall by any means hurt you.

GREEK WORDS

No Greek words were shown on the TV program.

SYNOPSIS

As we have noted throughout this series, the children of Israel had lived in Egypt as slaves for about 400 years. When God miraculously delivered them and brought them out into the wilderness so they could freely worship Him, they began to encounter things they hadn't faced for centuries. Wild animals, ferocious beasts, and foreign adversaries became a source of great fear.

It was in the midst of these trying circumstances that Moses penned the protective promises of Psalm 91, declaring to the people of God — both then and now — that if they would live in the shadow of Almighty God, they wouldn't need to fear anything because the Lord Himself would be their Guardian God!

The emphasis of this lesson:

When you're abiding in the shadow of the Almighty, God will empower you to tread on your enemies and advance into all He's called you to do. If you set your love upon Him and proclaim His promises to Him, He will deliver you and set you out of the enemy's reach. He will honor you greatly, demonstrate the fullness of His salvation, and give you long life.

A Final Review of Psalm 91:1

Once more, let's take a final look at Psalm 91:1, which declares, "He that dwelleth in the secret place of the most High shall abide under the shadow of the Almighty."

Understanding the Hebrew word for "dwelleth" here is pivotal. It means *to dwell, to lodge, to take up residency*, or *to move into a place and permanently stay there*. The words "secret place" describe *an inner chamber, a place of concealment, a hiding place*, or *a place of secrecy*. It is a Hebrew word denoting *the most secret compartment*.

For us as believers, our secret place is *in Christ*. According to First Corinthians 12:13, the moment we said *yes* to the Lordship of Jesus, instantly, the Holy Spirit grabbed us and placed us into the Body of Christ — the secret place. In fact, there's no place safer than being in Christ. We're told in Colossians 2:10 that we are complete in Him, and He is the head of all principality and power. This leads us back to Psalm 91:1 where it specifies that the secret place is of the *Most High*.

The Hebrew word for "Most High" is *Elyon*, and it means *The One Who Is Supreme*. Friend, that is Jesus! He is the Lord and has ultimate authority over all. As a Christian, you are tucked away deeply inside Him, if you have submitted to His Lordship.

Now, there are some people who got saved and walked closely with the Lord for quite some time. But due to various circumstances and challenges in their lives, they drifted away from the intimacy they once had. To be clear, the promises of Psalm 91 are not able to be claimed by people who once walked with the Lord but are now distant from Him. To claim these verses and see them activated in our life, we must stay in close fellowship with the Lord, abiding in the shadow of the Almighty.

As we have stated, the only way you can be in the shadow of the Almighty is if you're close to Him. Just as a person's shadow only goes so far, so does the Lord's shadow. If you don't move with Him — or move too far away from Him — you're going to move out of His shadow. The use of this shadow imagery in Psalm 91 infers that all its promises are not automatically granted to those who are saved. Rather, they are activated in the lives of the people who are devoted to the Lord and walk very close to Him — so close that they're living under His shadow.

The word "shadow" depicts *a shelter* or *a hiding place*. It also denotes *one who stays in step with the Lord*, which makes sense, given the fact that the verse speaks of *the shadow of the Almighty*. The word "Almighty" in Hebrew is *Shaddai*, and it depicts God as the *Great Provider* and *One Who Overpowers*. This tells us that if we're living in the shadow of the Almighty, His prosperity, His provision, and His protection will overcome us because we're living in His shadow.

You Will 'Tread Upon' and Advance Beyond Your Enemies

When we come to Psalm 91:13, we read, "Thou shalt tread upon the lion and adder: the young lion and the dragon shalt thou trample under feet." This passage is packed with revelation, beginning with the words "thou shalt tread." In the original Hebrew, this means *to advance, march, go forth, tread,* or *walk*. This lets us know that when we're abiding in the shadow of the Almighty, God not only empowers us to tread on our enemies, but He also enables us to *advance* into all that He's called us to do.

Again, the scripture says, "Thou shalt tread upon the lion and adder…" (Psalm 91:13). The word "upon" in Hebrew means *above, over,* or *upon.* "Lion" in Hebrew does describe *a lion,* but specifically it depicts *a fierce lion* that has come to attack. And the word "adder" describes *a venomous serpent,* possibly even a *cobra*. What's interesting is that this word is from a root word meaning *to twist*. Hence, it also denotes *a twisted attack or twisted situation* — something wild, bizarre, and that you'd never imagine to take place. Nevertheless, because you're living in the shadow of *Shaddai,* you have the ability to walk right over it!

The verse goes on to say that you also have the ability to tread upon and march beyond the attack of "the young lion and the dragon." In Hebrew, "young lion" simply means *a young lion that is hungry,* and the word "dragon" depicts *a dragon, monster, sea monster,* or *serpent* — all of which a traveler may encounter while taking a journey. Although we will likely not encounter a monster from a horror movie, we may encounter monstrous things that seek to victimize us.

But if we've taken up residency in the presence of God, the Bible says, "…Thou shalt trample [them] under foot" (Psalm 91:13). This phrase in Hebrew means *to stomp on, to trample,* or *to tread upon*. In other words, you may face a horrific situation, but because you're under the shadow of the

Almighty, you will stomp all over it and even advance in God's plans for your life.

This promise is echoed almost word for word by Jesus Himself in Luke 10:19 where He declared, "Behold, I give unto you power to tread on serpents and scorpions, and over all the power of the enemy: and NOTHING shall by any means hurt you."

Notice the word "behold," which opens the verse. It is the Greek word *idou*, which expresses *bewilderment, amazement,* and *awe*. It demonstrates the injection of Jesus' own feelings regarding what He is about to say. In fact, the word *idou* is the equivalent of Him saying, "Wow! It is shocking, amazing, and dumbfounding what I'm about to say to you! Listen!" And then He says:

> **...I give unto you power to tread on serpents and scorpions, and over all the power of the enemy: and NOTHING shall by any means hurt you.**
> — **Luke 10:19**

Interestingly, Jesus took the promise of being able to tread on serpents and scorpions and raised it to a higher level. He said He gave us power over *all the power of the enemy*, and nothing shall by any means harm us! WOW! Stop for a moment and say, "*Praise God!*" And how do we operate in this devil-stomping power? Psalm 91:1 tells us it's by abiding in the shadow of the Almighty. When we're walking close to the Lord, we're empowered to tread upon the lion and the adder, the young lion and the dragon.

Those Who Truly Love God, He Delivers

When we come to Psalm 91:14, the Lord Himself begins to speak and declare what He is going to do for all who have chosen to dwell in His shadow. He says, "Because he hath set his love upon me, therefore will I deliver him: I will set him on high, because he hath known my name."

For a second time, we see the word "because" at the opening of a verse, and again it points to the *result* of abiding in the shadow of the Almighty. It's God's way of saying, "This is the result of what happens to those who stay close to Me," or "Here's what I'm going to do for you because you continued to walk in My shadow, and you've set your love upon Me."

The phrase "set his love" in Hebrew means *to be attached*; *to delight*; *to be devoted*; or *to deeply love*. What this tells us is that when the Lord sees you doing your best to stay in step with Him and to stay in His shadow, He notices it and says, "Wow, that's a person who's deeply devoted and who's really trying to stay attached to Me." Indeed, God knows who's walking in His shadow and striving to obey Him, and those who are devoted to and deeply love the Lord, He will deliver.

What Is the Evidence That We've Set Our Love on the Lord?

Setting our love upon the Lord and choosing to be attached to Him is a personal choice, and it is often evidenced by the following:

- **Spending time regularly with God**
- **Praying and fellowshipping with Him**
- **Reading, studying, and meditating on His Word**
- **Worshiping the Lord — giving Him thanks and praise from a grateful heart**
- **Participating in the ministry and work of the Body of Christ**
- **Giving your tithes and offerings**

All these practices are proof that a person is really trying to abide in the shadow of the Almighty. Keep in mind that these are outward demonstrations of a heart that is totally devoted to God. Although we are not saved by what we do, when we are truly saved, our actions and activities show it.

The Lord Will 'Set Us on High'

And to those who set their love on the Lord, He said, "…Therefore will I deliver him: I will set him on high, because he hath known my name" (Psalm 91:14). In Hebrew, the phrase "therefore I will deliver him" means *to carry away from danger, to cause to escape,* or *to deliver*. It is the idea of enabling one to slip out of a bad, dangerous place.

In addition to delivering those who love Him, God said, "I will set him on high." In Hebrew, this means *to be inaccessibly high, out of reach,* or *inaccessible*. Thus, when we delight in and devote ourselves to the Lord and dwell in His magnificent shadow, He will elevate us out of the enemy's reach and make us inaccessible.

When you read the Psalms and the book of Proverbs, you will often see phrases like *the Lord will set me on high* or *the Lord will set me upon a rock*. These are references to God lifting us up high out of the reach of our enemies. When He sets us up on a rock — which is symbolic of Jesus Christ — our enemies can't reach us, even if they try! The Lord makes us inaccessible because we're dwelling in the shadow of the Almighty!

The Lord Answers and Delivers Us When We Call on Him and Proclaim His Promises

In Psalm 91:15, God goes on to say, "He shall call upon me, and I will answer him: I will be with him in trouble; I will deliver him, and honour him." In Hebrew, the phrase "he shall call upon me" means *to call, to proclaim*, or *to read*. In the context of this passage, it pictures one who proclaims the Lord's promises and calls out to Him for help. It is as if God is saying, "The one who calls out to Me and proclaims My promises back to Me, I will answer him."

Next, God says, "I will answer him." In Hebrew, this literally means, *"I will respond to him."* When the Lord's protective promises are in your mouth and you're abiding in fellowship with Him, He will cause His promises to be activated and come to pass in your life.

The Lord then promises, "…I will be with him in trouble…" (Psalm 91:15). What's interesting here is that the original Hebrew text is much stronger. It says, *"With him I will be."* Specifically, God guarantees to be with those who love Him and are "in trouble." This phrase is a translation of the Hebrew word meaning *in adversity, in difficulty, in distress, in straits*, or *in tribulation*.

By abiding in the shadow of the Almighty and understanding His Name, God promises to be with us *in trouble* and "deliver" us. In Hebrew, the phrase "I will deliver him" means *God will draw us out [of a situation] — He will deliver us* or *loosen us from bonds*. When we set our love on the Lord, know His Name, and abide in His shadow, He will draw us out of bad situations and set us free.

The Lord Greatly Honors Us and 'Satisfies' Us With Long Life

The Lord then adds, "…And [I will] honor him" (Psalm 91:15). Interestingly, the word "honor" means *to be heavy or weighty*. Hence, this passage pictures *one who is heavily loaded with honor*. Rather than being a small honor, God greatly honors the one who abides in His shadow and sets his love and affection on Him.

Psalm 91 closes with the Lord declaring, "With long life will I satisfy him, and shew him my salvation" (v. 16). The word "long" here is a translation of a Hebrew word that *speaks of length*; thus, implying *longevity*. And the word "life" in Hebrew denotes *days*. As a phrase, "long life" depicts *long days* or *a very long life*.

Again, the Lord says, "With long life will I satisfy him…" (Psalm 91:16). In Hebrew, the words "will I satisfy him" mean *to have enough, to have plenty of,* or *to be fully satisfied.* To all those who are abiding in the Lord's shadow, the Lord promises that we can live until we are *satisfied*. Some people say that a full life span is 70 or 80 years, and they base it on Moses' words in Psalm 90:10. However, that verse was God's promise to the disobedient children of Israel living in the wilderness.

The truth is, God doesn't limit His blessing of long life to 70 or 80 years — or even 120 years as some people claim today. To be biblically accurate, Psalm 91:16 says God will honor you with a long life and satisfy you, which indicates that He'll give you as many years as you want until you're satisfied.

When Abraham breathed his last breath, the Bible says he was "full of years." Amazingly, he had lived 175 years and was satisfied (*see* Genesis 25:7,8). In the same way, God promises that we can live until we are satisfied and then depart in peace. The promise of long life is available to anyone who abides under the shadow of the Almighty.

The Lord Will Fully Demonstrate His Salvation to Us

God's final words in Psalm 91:16 are: "…And [I will] shew him my salvation." In Hebrew, the phrase "and shew him" means *to behold, experience, see, or fully view.* This infers *a full demonstration*, and in the context of this verse, it is the equivalent of God saying, "To the one living in My shadow and staying close to Me, I will fully demonstrate My salvation. He will see and experience every aspect of it."

This brings us to the word "salvation," which in Hebrew includes every form of salvation, including *deliverance, healing, preservation, prosperity,* and *overall welfare that touches every realm of life.* Thus, this salvation is not just about being eternally saved and going to Heaven. It's about experiencing His life-giving blessings in this present life as well.

Friend, all the promises of Psalm 91 belong to anyone who chooses to abide in the shadow of the Almighty — to anyone who knows and understands the Lord's Name and proclaims His promises to Him. So make the decision to live in step with the Lord and abide in His presence daily. Put His promises in your mouth and speak them to the Lord and over your life. He will activate them in your life and satisfy you with the kind of abundant life you never knew was possible!

STUDY QUESTIONS

> Study to shew thyself approved unto God, a workman that
> needeth not to be ashamed, rightly dividing the word of truth.
> — 2 Timothy 2:15

1. Just before going to the Cross, Jesus told us the importance of "abiding in the vine." Carefully reflect on His words, which are recorded in John 15:1-8, and identify who is the *vine*, who are the *branches*, and who is the *Vinedresser* or *Gardener*. How is Jesus' illustration here similar to "abiding in the shadow of the Almighty"? How is it different?

2. Jesus said, "Behold, I give unto you power to tread on serpents and scorpions, and over all the power of the enemy: and *nothing* shall by any means hurt you" (Luke 10:19). What other kinds of *power* and *authority* did Jesus say He gave us? Dive into these verses for the answers:
   - John 1:12,13; 1 John 3:1,2 _____
   - Matthew 16:19 and 18:18 _____
   - Matthew 18:19,20 _____
   - John 14:13,14 _____
   - Mark 16:17,18 _____

PRACTICAL APPLICATION

> But be ye doers of the word, and not hearers only,
> deceiving your own selves.
> — James 1:22

1. As you finish this series of lessons on Psalm 91, what are your top two takeaways that you really want to remember? Why are these so impactful to you?
2. The evidence of setting our love upon the Lord includes: spending time with Him regularly; praying and fellowshipping with Him; reading, studying, and meditating on His Word; worshiping Him and thanking Him from a grateful heart; participating in the ministry of the Body of Christ; and giving our tithes and offerings. On a scale of 1 to 5 (5 being great and 1 being very insufficient), how would you rate yourself in these areas? How do you think God would rate you? Pray and ask Him for the power and desire to come up higher in the areas where you're falling short.
3. Are the protective promises of God active in your life? Are you experiencing the overflow of His power, provision, and protection? Are you trampling your enemies under foot and advancing in the plans and purpose God has for your life? If you answered *no* to any of these questions, take time to pray and ask the Lord, "Am I still abiding close to You in Your shadow? Or have I drifted so far away from You that I can no longer claim Your promises? Please show me what's going on in my life and what adjustments I need to make to return to abiding in Your shadow. In Jesus' name. Amen."

CLAIM YOUR FREE RESOURCE!

As a way of introducing you further to the teaching ministry of Rick Renner, we would like to send you FREE of charge his teaching, "How To Receive a Miraculous Touch From God" on CD or as an MP3 download.

In His earthly ministry, Jesus commonly healed *all* who were sick of *all* their diseases. In this profound message, learn about the manifold dimensions of Christ's wisdom, goodness, power, and love toward all humanity who came to Him in faith with their needs.

☑ YES, I want to receive Rick Renner's monthly teaching letter!

Simply scan the QR code to claim this resource or go to:
renner.org/claim-your-free-offer

Connect WITH US!

renner.org

- facebook.com/rickrenner • facebook.com/rennerdenise
- youtube.com/rennerministries • youtube.com/deniserenner
- instagram.com/rickrrenner • instagram.com/rennerministries_ instagram.com/rennerdenise

Made in the USA
Middletown, DE
26 June 2024